Imam Muhammad Shirazi

War, Peace and Non-violence

An Islamic perspective

Co-Publisher

Tahrike Tarsile Qur'an, Inc.

Publishers and Distributors of Holy Qur'an
80-08 51st Avenue
Elmhurst, New York 11373
E-mail: orders@koranusa.org
http://www.koranusa.org

fountain books
BM Box 8545
London WC1N 3XX
UK
www.fountainbooks.co.uk

Co-Publisher
Tahrike Tarsile Qur'an, Inc.
Publishers and Distributors of Holy Qur'an
80-08 51st Avenue
Elmhurst, New York 11373
E-mail: orders@koranusa.org
http://www.koranusa.org

First U.S. Edition 2001

Library of Congress Catalog Number:
British Library Cataloguing in Publication Data

ISBN: 1-879402-83-1 English

Printed in Canada

Table of Contents

In the Name of Allah, The Beneficent The Merciful.
All Praise is to Him, Lord of the Worlds.
Let Allah's Blessings be upon Muhammad
and upon his righteous and pure family.

Part One

In addressing the issue of universal peace, the author in this discourse begins with tackling the phenomenon of war by discussing aspects such as the causes of war, as well as the management of war and behaviour during war. The author goes on to present some of the Islamic perspective on war and the measures needed to contain war and its causes. The following is Chapter 4 of Imam Shirazi's book ***The New Order for a World of Faith, Freedom, Prosperity, and Peace*** pp349-402.

Translated by Ali Adam.

Islam's View on War

War is the worst thing known to mankind

War is the worst thing known to mankind throughout his long history. It brings about the killing and maiming of human beings, the loss of their powers and their disfigurement. It also causes the destruction of civilisations, stirs up hatred and resentments amongst people, and passes psychological problems on to future generations. It also causes the fighters to become prisoners of war. For these reasons, war must be avoided at all costs and if war becomes necessary – because the enemy has forced the situation – it is imperative that war should be limited to the least degree of necessity. It is also imperative that humanity in general put an end to wars finally so that they do not occur in the future.

War is an illness

War has been a phenomenon from the earliest times. It is said that it is confirmed as a fact in the Holy Qur'an in the verse:

{And had Allah not checked one set of people by means of another, the Earth would indeed be full of corruption.} [1]

Some say that war is one manifestation of the struggle for survival which is a natural attribute of all living things and which will never cease, and that it is one of the traditions of human society. However, the prevention of war by finding another solution is what should be sought. For illness and disease is also a human reality from the very beginning as is the burning of cities, houses and shops or destruction by flooding and other natural events, which can cause harm to humanity. However, all of this does not make war inevitable, for war is not a prime reality but rather a secondary phenomenon, which happens because of the malice of certain individuals.

Hence, a group of religious scholars have said that war in itself is bad and ugly because it entails the killing of people and destruction. The Holy Qur'an supports this in the following verse:

{Fighting is prescribed upon you though ye dislike it. But it is possible that you dislike a thing that is good for you and that you

[1] *The Holy Qur'an*: The Heifer (2): 251.

love a thing that is bad for you. Allah knoweth and you knoweth not.} [2]

On the surface, this verse shows that if fighting were a natural thing then Allah would not have said: **{though ye dislike it.}**. Therefore, war is a social phenomenon brought about by corrupt instincts and not something natural in humanity.

War as the last resort

We find that the Prophet Muhammad *(S)*[3] did not instigate a single war, but rather made war only in self-defence. Even then he did not resort to defensive wars until after the exhaustion of a number of alternatives:

Firstly neutrality, as this was the case between the Prophet (S) and Abyssinia. Neutrality is the first phase of non-aggression. After neutrality comes the turn of the treaty of non-aggression as practised by the Prophet (S) when he entered into a treaty with the Jews of Madinah or when he entered into a treaty with the non-believers of Makkah at Hudaibia.

Islam through conviction

After these two possibilities comes the role of Islam. For if the other party (the enemy) accepts Islam he will have spared his wealth and blood and there will be no enmity other than for the wrongdoers and oppressors. The acceptance of Islam is clearly not a matter for compulsion it rather consists of solid evidences, which promote the conviction of the intellect in the matters of the beginning and the resurrection, the Prophet (S) and the Sacred Law etc.

The Jizyah tax . . . finally

In the absence of neutrality, or a treaty, or the acceptance of Islam, then the *'Jizyah'* tax[4] comes into play as was practised by the Prophet (S) with the Christians of Najran. The 'Jizyah' tax is of two types:

---

[2] *The Holy Qur'an*: The Heifer (2): 216.
[3] *Sall-Allah Alayhi wa Alihi wa Sallam*, meaning Peace and Blessings of Allah be upon him and his infallible family. This is always stated after the mention of the name of the Prophet out of respect for the Prophet of Islam (S).

1. The '*Jizyah*' of the people of the '*Dhimma*' or protectorate who live under the auspices of Islam. This tax is taken from them in the same way that the '*Khums*' and '*Zakat*' taxes are taken from the Muslims. We have mentioned in our books of jurisprudence that the '*Jizyah*' tax is taken solely from the unbelievers (contrary to what is widely believed). The money collected from the unbelievers who live under the province of Islam does not come under the heading of '*Khums*' or '*Zakat*' but rather under the heading of the '*Jizyah*' tax. This applies whether the unbelievers are 'People of the Book' like Jews or Christians or Zoroastrians, or others like the Idolaters or the Polytheists.

2. The '*Jizyah*' tax collected from those unbelievers who are not under the auspices of Islam. This is collected because of the obduracy of those to whom the truth has appeared, as the Prophet (S) did with the Christians of Najran when he discussed with their learned men the truthfulness of Islam but they dismissed it. The Prophet (S) then disputed further with them but they still resisted. After that there was nothing left but their obstinacy. The obstinate person should become less obstinate in the face of what should return him gradually to the truth.

Allah states in the Qur'an regarding the Christians of Najran:

{The similitude of Jesus in the sight of Allah is as that of Adam, He created him from pure earth then said to him 'Be', and so he was. This is the truth from your Lord so do not be amongst the doubters. And if anyone disputes with you in this matter after knowledge has come to you, say: 'Come let us gather together our sons and your sons, our wives and your wives, ourselves and yourselves, then let us earnestly pray and invoke the curse of Allah upon the liars.' This is the true account: there is no god but Allah, and Allah is indeed The Exalted in Power, The Wise. But if they turn back, Allah has full knowledge of those who cause mischief. Say: ' O People of the Book! Come to a common parlance between us and you: that we worship none but Allah and we associate no partners with Him and we take no lords from amongst ourselves instead of Allah. But if they turn back then say: Bear witness that we are Muslims.} [5]

---

[4] The *Jizyah* tax is paid by the non-Muslims, as opposed to the *Khums* and *Zakat* taxes paid by the Muslims.

[5] *The Holy Qur'an*: The Family of 'Emran (3): 59–64.

The Prophet's wars were fought in self defence

When all these aforementioned ways and means have been exhausted, then comes the turn of the defensive war. All the wars of the Prophet (S) were of this nature. For example, the first clash of the Muslims with the Qureish occurred when the raiding party of 'Abdullah ibn Jahsh came up against the caravans of the Qureish which were coming from al-Sham (Syria) led by Abu Sufyan. This was a retort to the aggression of the Polytheists against the Prophet (S) and his companions, which had gone on for ten years. They had killed some of them, banished some to Abyssinia and some to Madinah, and tortured another group of them and destroyed the honour of others as in the account of Sumayyaha the mother of 'Ammar. They confiscated their houses and their wealth in Makkah. And if this was not enough, they approached the other Arabian tribes, which surrounded Madinah and bribed them not to let the Prophet's caravans pass through their lands. This threatened the Muslims with death by starvation. The defensive economic blockade is one legal method used in wars, and what the Muslims wanted from this raiding party and what followed it (like the battle of Badr) was to place an economic blockade on the people of Makkah who were at war with the Prophet in the same way that they had placed a blockade upon him.

As for the rest of the Prophet's raids, wars and assaults, they resulted from either a breaking of the treaty by the other side as did the Jews of the clan of Qainaqa' in Madinah, and the Polytheists of the Qureish in breaking the peace treaty of Hudaibia, or they were to repel the enemy as in the battles of Uhud and al-Khandaq. Otherwise they were for defensive purposes as in the story of Mu'ta when the Persians and the Romans had engaged in aggression towards the Islamic state and Islam was surrounded by enemies who only sought the worst for Islam. They began to try to attack Islam and tear it out by the roots and kill the Prophet (S) and exterminate the Muslims. They indeed began to do this. Hercules, the leader of the Romans killed a group of his subjects who had become Muslims in Syria. All of this gave the Prophet (S) the religious, common law, and legal right to defence. Likewise with the Persians, Khosrau their leader ordered his governor in Yemen to send some of his henchmen to bring him the blessed head of the Prophet. However the messengers who came to Madinah refused when they saw the Muslims thronging around the Prophet who reasoned with them in a story much mentioned in the chronicles.

The least amount of casualties

The Prophet (S) used to strive to keep the amount of killing and prisoners in his wars to a bare minimum in a way that the world has not witnessed either prior to or after the advent of Islam. For example, one writer mentions that the number of people killed on both sides (Muslims and Polytheists) in all the battles in which the Prophet fought did not exceed much more than one thousand and this in more than eighty wars. Another mentions that the number killed in all the wars was 1018 people. A third mentions that the number of Infidels and Muslims killed in all the wars was no more than 1400 this being the largest number mentioned in this regard. Dr. Muhammad Hamidullah in his book 'Muhammad' mentions that the Prophet Muhammad (S), although he gained control of more than one million square miles of territory which is equal to all of Europe excluding Russia, and although millions of people lived in this area, only one-hundred and fifty Muslims were killed in all of his wars. He adds that this number amounts to approximately one death per month. This is only due to the respect that Islam has for blood and its avoidance of killing wherever possible.

Excess of killing and torturing

In contrast to the government of the Prophet (S) we find that most other governments went to excesses in blood spilling. Historians say that the Assyrians were cruel and heartless. They would destroy cities, which they conquered after besieging them, and would go to great lengths in killing, torture, and mutilations. They would reward the army for every severed head brought from the battlefield. They would set about killing all the prisoners of war on the battlefield when they were great in number so that they would not consume food and drink, or be a danger to the rear of the army. The kings and leaders would lead the carnage and would begin it by putting out the eyes and cutting the throats of prisoners. The leaders and nobles amongst the prisoners would be tortured before being killed. Their ears and noses would be amputated, their tongues cut out and their hands and feet severed or they would be skinned alive or roasted over fire or thrown from high towers. The king who ascended the throne of Assyria in the year 745 B.C. used to crucify prisoners on posts while archers would kill them with arrows. In certain wars he would use prisoners to pull carriages laden with wood instead of beasts of burden.

Frightening scenes of the brutality of the Moguls

In the book 'Prisoners of War' in the story of the Moguls the writer says:

> "The Moguls were known for cruelty, brutality and bloodshed. Genghis Khan the founder of their empire was famous for violence, killing, and his love of destruction and annihilation. Amongst their wars they became embroiled with the Kharazm Shah 'Ala al-Din. The Moguls burned the city of Bukhara and plundered its wealth and raped the women. The prisoners were marched to the city of Samarqand. When they could not keep up with the horsemen Genghis Khan ordered that anyone who lagged behind be killed and Bukhara was razed to the ground. Samarqand met with the same fate when the city was plundered and the inhabitants killed and 30,000 skilled craftsmen were taken prisoner. Genghis Khan sent them to his sons in the north. A great number were forcibly enlisted into the army and used for military operations and transport.
>
> In Khorasan, the Moguls gathered the citizens in a wide space and ordered them to manacle one another. They then began to slaughter them killing more than 70,000. When they occupied Merv, they distributed its occupants amongst the Mongol warriors each of whom got a share. They only spared 400 people who fulfilled the needs of the army and some individuals were taken as slaves. The rest of the cities met with the same fate. When the Moguls heard that some citizens were sleeping amongst the corpses of those killed the order was given that every head should be severed from its body, an order that they carried out in all future battles. They would pursue those who fled like hunters pursuing their prey. They would use all kinds of devices to bring people out from their hiding places. For example they forced a muezzin from amongst the prisoners to give the call to prayer so the Muslims came out from concealment believing that the raiders had left but they were ambushed and wiped out. Before they left the cities they would burn produce and crops so that those who were hiding or had fled would die of hunger.
>
> The policy of Genghis Khan in his wars was to slaughter all of the soldiers in the garrisons and the inhabitants of the cities and to plunder and pillage and drown the prisoners. If a city resisted the Moguls they would do even worse to it. The city of Nisapur

resisted for a few days and its reward was the wholesale slaughter of men, women, and children.

The Moguls did in Russia what they did in the state of Kharazm, destroying and burning. They took a number of Russian leaders prisoners through deception and betrayal and put them in chains. Then carpets were put over them and the Mongol leaders sat upon them to eat the victory banquet while the Russian leaders were dying of suffocation.

The Moguls then returned to Mongolia and destroyed the city of Bulghar, and pillaged all the cities of Bazan and razed their buildings to the ground and burned Moscow and besieged Tlotir. When the noblemen cut their hair and hid in churches and wore the robes of monks, the Moguls ordered that the church and the city be burnt and all perished. Hulagu continued the advance in western Asia until he reached Tabriz and turned towards Baghdad the seat of the 'Abbasid leadership. They laid siege to Baghdad for forty days and set up mangonels around all the castles and fortresses. Then they pelted them with rocks and flaming torches making a large breach in the walls and setting fire to houses.

When the Caliph saw that there was no way out except through peace he requested peace and showed his readiness to surrender on condition that his life and the lives of the citizens be spared. He went out to meet Hulagu with three thousand judges, aides and nobles. But Hulagu betrayed the agreement and double-crossed them and destroyed the city. He ordered that the city be pillaged and the population slaughtered. The bodies of those pleading for help fell under the hooves of the horses and the women were raped. The blood flowed in the streets for three days until the waters of the Tigris were red for a number of miles. The city became a free for all for six weeks. They slaughtered the population, violated sacred sites, burned houses, palaces were levelled, and mosques and tombs were ruined by fire or pickaxes. The patients in the hospitals were slaughtered, students and professors were killed in the schools. The shrines of saints and Imams were desecrated and the corpses burnt. The bloodbath went on for a number of days until Baghdad became a wasteland of rubble. More than a million and a half citizens had perished. The Moguls then crossed the Euphrates heading towards the Arabian Peninsula in pursuit of the populace. They killed and pillaged and destroyed all the population of al-Raha, Jaran, and

Nasibayn and butchered in Aleppo fifty thousand and abused ten thousand women and children.

They did the same thing in all the lands of Islam. For example when Tamburlaine heard of the killing of a number of his men and soldiers in Isfahan he became angry and ordered his army to invade the city and that each soldier was to return with the head of one of the citizens who had been killed which the army duly did. The city became a human bloodbath. By the evening some 70,000 of the victims skulls had piled up so Tamburlaine ordered that towers be built from them in the streets. The same thing happened in other cities they reached, slaughtering the populace and setting fire to the cities."

Modern wars are no less brutal

We find the situation in modern wars to be the same if not worse than that. America with the atomic bomb killed more than 250,000 people in Japan in the space of hours, and burnt everything.

When the British came to Iraq, they treated the people in the worst possible ways. They would kill the wounded and be merciless towards the prisoners and would extract corpses from the graves desiring the shirts and clothes. In Sudan, the British soldiers would cut off the heads of those killed and send them to London to be made into ashtrays out of hatred for the Muslims.

In Libya, the Italians killed half the populace, which in those days reached a million. They killed half a million in the most horrible ways. They would use corpses as an example to the rest and would torture the living foully.

Likewise the French in Algeria where they killed a million out of nine million people. Some statistics say that the killed two millions. They would use corpses as an example and would torture the living cruelly in a way that has few equals.

In the war between India and East Pakistan (Bangladesh) more than three millions were killed through hunger, torture or plague.

The Russians killed five million Muslims in various ways like burning, drowning, torturing to death and shooting in Tajikistan, Turkmenistan and the other Islamic lands which they took control of. They also killed more than one million in Afghanistan and filled their prisons with innocent people and tortured the people in the most disgusting ways.

The Americans in Vietnam and elsewhere have killed a vast number of people counted in millions. They also used to torture people and destroy crops.

The world witnesses in the modern age the worst forms of killing, torture, and burning and the degradation of the nobility of the human being. The events of the first and second world wars are well known and to be found documented in books.

The increase of the dangers of war in the modern age

In a previous book of ours *"Sociology"*[6] regarding the dangers of war we have written: 'It is imperative that the nations strive in all earnestness to bring about a comprehensive peace in our time, for the dangers of war have increased in a way unimaginable. This increase has brought about a number of considerations:

The weapons of mass destruction that science has discovered and the use of these weapons in wars bring about the devastation of civilisation whether that be in limited wars or world wars, for even limited wars cause destruction on their own scale. For example, in the Lebanese war 150,000 people were killed or injured. In the Iran-Iraq war the number of dead and injured has been estimated at more than 1,500,000 and the losses due to the war at 500 billion dollars. If, God forbid, a world war was to occur, then it is likely that civilisation would end. A report has mentioned that it was the plan of America to destroy in a nuclear attack 85 per cent of Russia's manufacturing plants. Each of America and Russia have stockpiled enough weapons of mass destruction to destroy humanity seven times over. There are bombs, which if dropped on a city would annihilate everything in an area of 250 square miles. There are other fearsome weapons of mass destruction which when compared with the weapons of the second world war are like the cannon and tank in comparison with primitive weapons like the sword and the spear.

[6] *Al-Fiqh* series, volumes 109-110.

The other effects of war

War, in addition to the death and destruction has other effects:

1. It leaves behind war wounded and disabled people who will suffer from their complaints for the rest of their lives. The weapons of mass destruction cause many different diseases and disfigurements in humanity, animals, and to the land itself. There is a report that Russia bought 25 million prosthetic limbs and organs like hands, legs, and eyes for the maimed after the end of the Second World War. This in addition to the fact that atomic warfare irradiates houses and causes plants not to grow in the earth for long periods of time.

2. War eats into the economy on a great scale. States change their apparatus during time of war to the apparatus of war which gobbles up money and brings about poverty for many years. Gustav Le Bon has mentioned that Spain has not yet recovered from the Crusades against the Muslims and this is after nearly 1000 years. Another historian has said that Iraq has not recovered from its destruction at the hands of the Moguls seven centuries ago. America spent 7.4% of its GNP on the cold war in the year 1953. If this were the case for the cold war what would be the case for the hot war? In addition to the warring nations, war eats into the economy of all the other nations, for these days the economy is not confined to one place on earth but the economy of all nations has become interconnected and goods are imported and exported to and from all states. Even the nations that are nominally neutral but are not really neutral are affected economically by war. All can remember how the world fell into dire straits during the second world war in both the nations at war and those not at war.

3. War also causes a decline in civilisation for the warring nations and those connected to them and indeed all the nations of the world. For when every nation becomes at war then cultural services, manufacturing, agriculture, and education cease on a large scale which causes the stagnation of the culture and indeed its decline. A great number of different types of scholars who are the axis of the progress of the civilisation can become taken up by the war. Certain newspapers have mentioned that Egypt lost ten thousand engineers, experts and doctors when the Israeli Bar-Levi line was destroyed.

Towards a comprehensive peace

It is then necessary, for the sake of a general and comprehensive peace, to transfer the weapons making factories into those of peaceful motives. It should not be argued that warfare provides work for millions of workers for many of these workers could be absorbed by works with peaceful intent. Projects for the housing, health and the other needs of the people of the world could be put into action as well as projects to conquer space. If it was inevitable that a surplus of workers were left without any work this does not necessitate that they be idle. They can occupy themselves with seeking knowledge or in acts of worship or in recreation after the work had been distributed to them and others.

For example, let us suppose that there are ten million workers each one occupied eight hours per day in the different areas of manufacturing and agriculture and half of them – five million – were working in the arms industry. If they were put to work in works of a peaceful nature there might remain two million without any work the other three million being absorbed by the works of a peaceful motive. In this case the available work could be distributed amongst the ten million and the length of the working day reduced. So in the example given, rather than having ten million working eight hours per day so that five million may work in the arms industry, each worker would work six and two fifths hours per day and for the rest of the time they could spend it in science and knowledge - teaching or learning or experimenting, or in acts of worship which bring about the good in this life and the next, or with recreation like travelling etc.

It is not right to say that we should manufacture weapons and kill the people just so that there is no unemployment. It is as if there was a family half of whom had work and half of whom did not and we said that the half who did not have work should occupy themselves in killing the other half who do have work just so that the half who did not have work were busy doing something. This kind of logic is neither reasonable nor lawful; it is nothing but corrupt.

It is necessary then for us to bring forth peaceful work for the workers in arms factories as well as for those who are occupied in military matters like the officers, leaders, and soldiers and others. Naturally, there should remain a small number for possible emergencies, and the others if trained should be trained to an extent and will form a reserve army rather than a full time one. We have already mentioned in other books that Iran, in the days of the reformer al-Shirazi and the story of the prohibition of tobacco, had around ten million reserve soldiers – all of the population – and ten thousand men at arms for the times of peace. In any case, it is imperative that the problem of war be solved in this way or in another way. This is as regards the amount of weapons.

As regards to the type of weapons, it is imperative that weapons be reduced. That is, there should be committees to change the advanced weapons into light weapons like the rifle, then to substitute these light weapons for primitive weapons like the sword and the spear for it is a grave error for humanity to prepare weapons which will annihilate both the fighter and his enemy.

This is possible if we enable a general mobilisation for peace. Then the arms factories will become obsolete and the workers can be employed in other fields. Large armies will be demobilised and complicated weapons will be destroyed and there will be a return to light weapons. It is likely that the world will end with the sword as a weapon for it is found in certain traditions about the Imam al-Mahdi[7] (May Allah hasten his appearance) that he will carry a sword and in some accounts it will be the sword '*Dhulfiqar*' the same as was carried by *Amir-ul-Mu'mineen* Imam 'Ali ibn Abu Talib *(A)*[8] in the battles of Islam. It is related in some *hadith* that this sword descended from the heavens upon the Messenger of Allah (S). He then gave it to Imam 'Ali (A) after which it became part of the sacred inheritance of the impeccable Imams peace be upon them until it ended up with the Imam al-Mahdi (A). It is also found in the *hadith* that the area of the battle of the Imam and his companions will be between Makkah and al-Kufa, a very small area indeed. As for the rest of the lands, they will unite under the flag of the Imam without warfare.

Cutting the roots of war

In our book *'al-Fiqh series: Sociology'* we have said that the maintenance of peace is not possible through only the media and peace organisations, for peace is not merely a superficial issue just as war is not a superficial issue. The roots of war must be cut so that peace reigns. The roots of war are **human deprivation,** which brings about revolution

---

[7] Al-Mahdi, the Guided, the Saviour. The Prophet (S) promised that al-Mahdi will appear to spread peace and justice throughout the world after it has been filled with tyranny and oppression. Imam al-Mahdi is the twelfth, and last, infallible Imam from the household of the Prophet Muhammad (S).

[8] Alayh-es-Salam meaning peace be upon him. This is always stated after the mention of the name of one the infallible Imams out of respect for the Imam (A).

against the group causing this deprivation. The causes of this deprivation are **colonialism, exploitation, and despotism in government, in economics, or in science and education.** It is necessary for one seeking to sever the roots of war to prevent those who stir up war from attaining their goals and this through spreading political, economic, and social awareness. Political awareness brings about the non-surrender and defiance of people to dictators whether the dictatorship be open like inherited and *coupe de tat* governments or disguised like the governments who claim to Democracy but are in fact in the claws of Capitalism or of the single party like America, Britain, France, Russia, and China.

Economic awareness prevents the capital from being in the hands of a certain group whether that group has control of government as well - as in the former Soviet Union, or not – as in America.

Social awareness brings about the knowledge of the equality of society regarding education, power, and wealth. Indeed:

{Every person is responsible for what he has earned.} [9]

{Man will get only that for which he has strived.} [10]

It also brings about the knowledge that there is no 'chosen' class. If it is seen that education is particular to a certain group because they are wealthy or have power or are the ruling political party then it will be known that the society is corrupt and that it must be realigned until education is general to everyone. The same should be said for power and wealth.

The world has begun to head gradually towards this kind of awareness. The world power was held for a time in the hands of Britain, then America, then between the two powers America and Russia. However, the power now is distributed amongst a larger number of states – America, Russia, Europe, and China. It is true that in the area of military strength there are only two powers but there are numerous other centres of power in the political arena each of which has a treaty organisation. In the economic arena there are the two main states as well as Western Europe, China and Japan. In the nuclear field there is India and other states which has caused the world to come out gradually from being under a monopoly.

---

[9] *The Holy Qur'an*: The Mountain of Sinai (52): 21.
[10] *The Holy Qur'an*: The Star (53): 39.

Communism began to break up because of the splitting of China and the attempted split of Poland and the unrest of other states under the banner of Communism. It has also brought great ignominy upon itself, particularly when it invaded Hungary, Czechoslovakia, and Afghanistan.

Capitalism has begun to break up bit by bit. Both Japan and France have lost their empires, and British and American colonialism have here and there started tottering, especially in the Middle East, with the advent of the dirty policies of the state of Israel.

To continue, it has become an easier matter to increase the awareness of humanity. It is true that neutrality is not possible nor would it be correct, as a person should not stay silent in front of the oppressor. However, uneasy awareness has begun to work to bring about the proper kind of neutrality. As for the neutrality of twenty years ago, it was in reality a camouflage for agents of other regimes. For was Castro the agent of the east non-aligned? Or was Nasser the agent of America non-aligned?

In any case, an increase in awareness is required so that the roots of war may be extirpated; the roots being the confinement of knowledge and education, power, and wealth in the hands of a minority in the face of a deprived majority. This awareness as well as putting these three things in the hands of all will also bring people closer together and will create more relationships. Then corrupt partisans may not exploit the rest of humanity for their own personal goals. It is our opinion that whenever awareness increases nationalisms and corrupt group loyalties decrease in importance and matters of race, colour and geographical area are buried.

Exposing 'War by proxy'

It is also imperative before reaching the final result of a comprehensive peace to expose 'wars by proxy' and prevent them from occurring by a number of means:

a. Changing the relationships between the smaller states and the larger states so that the larger cannot make the smaller proxy in wars as is the custom now.

b. Exposing the military bases of the large states on the land of the smaller states.

c. Exposing the military pacts amongst the small states, which are under the sphere of influence of the large state, and making it clear that the small states in the pact only want the services of the larger states.

d. Strengthening the relations between neighbouring states so that the large states may not cause a war to occur between them.

e. (Most importantly) Bringing about the awareness of the people of the smaller nations so that they do not become as puppets in the hands of their governments which execute the orders of their masters.

It is indeed imperative that awareness is brought about for the people of nations in general so that they do not fall victim to the greed of Capitalists and Dictatorial rulers be they open Dictators like the former Soviet Union, or Dictators clothed in the flimsy robe of Democracy like Britain, France and America. It is these two groups – Dictators and Capitalists – who ignite wars always, backed up by corrupt religious scholars, or civilian experts.

The Messenger of Allah (S) spoke truly when he says:

> *'There are two groups from my nation who if righteous, my nation will be righteous and if corrupt, my nation will be corrupt.'*

He was asked: Who are they? O Messenger of Allah.' He said: *'The scholars and the commanders.'*

The Messenger of Allah (S) did not mention wealth in this *hadith* as it had a very small role in the past before the appearance of the corrupt capitalistic practices that play no part in Islam in the least. Those who ignited wars then were corrupt commanders and counterfeiting scholars who used to collaborate in oppressing the populace. Hence the Prophet (S) was alerted to the dangers of these two groups. It should also be made clear that the Prophet (S) was alerted in Islam to the danger of wealth only *"revolving amongst the rich."* We have discussed this topic in the chapter on wealth.

War is an extraordinary situation

Islam calls to peace and considers peace to be normal and war to be extraordinary and exceptional emergency entered into only out of desperation and as a last resort. Allah Almighty says:

{O ye who have faith, enter into peace all of you, and do not follow the footsteps of Satan.} [11]

{And if they incline to peace then incline to peace and put your trust in Allah.} [12]

{They will not cease from fighting you until they cause you to turn away from your religion if they are able.} [13]

{There was in them indeed an excellent example for you to follow of one who seeks Allah and the last day. But if any turn away, then know that Allah is Free of all wants, Worthy of all praise. It may be that Allah will establish friendship between you and those whom ye hold as your enemies. Allah has power, and Allah is Oft Forgiving, Most Merciful. Allah does not forbid you from dealing kindly and justly with those who do not fight you for your religion or drive you from your homes. Allah loveth those who are just. Allah only forbids you from taking as allies those who fight you for your religion and turn you out from your homes and aid others in turning you out from your homes. Whoever takes them as allies, they are the wrongdoers.} [14]

So we can see that Islam orders that those who persist in fighting the Muslims and seek enmity be fought back, and prohibits making friends with these types of people. As for those people who do not fight the believers or expel them from their homes, Allah indicates that they should be treated kindly and with fairness even though they may be infidels.

There are many other Qur'anic verses which if collected would show that *jihad* and war are secondary and extraordinary and that peace is the primary ruling as we have already indicated.

In a *hadith*, *Amir-ul-Mu'mineen* Imam 'Ali (A) spoke to his troops before meeting the enemy at the battle of Siffin:

> *"Do not fight them until they begin to fight, for you by the grace of Allah have the just cause, and by leaving them until they start on you, you will have another just cause over them."*

---

[11] *The Holy Qur'an*: The Heifer (2): 208.
[12] *The Holy Qur'an*: Public Estates (8): 61.
[13] *The Holy Qur'an*: The Heifer (2): 217.
[14] *The Holy Qur'an*: The Woman Tested (60): 6-9.

In a letter, Imam Ali (A) relates what took place in the battle of Siffin:

> *"Initially, it was that we and the group from the people of Syria (the army of Mu'awiyah) faced one other on the battlefield. It is obvious (for both sides) that our Lord is One and our Prophet is one and our call to Islam is one and we do not seek to increase their faith in Allah and belief in His Prophet nor do they seek to increase ours. Everything is common between us except for our difference over the blood of 'Uthman in which we are innocent. So we said: Come let us solve what may not be achieved today by extinguishing the uprising and calming the general populace so that the rule may become firm and consolidated. Then we will become stronger in putting the truth in its rightful place. They said: 'No, we will solve it by seeing who will have the upper hand in battle and they refused all but war. When both them and us had been torn by war and it had put its claws in them and us, then they responded to that which we had called them to previously. We accepted this and hurried to meet their requests so that they might have no complaint or cause against us."*

He also said to his son al-Hassan: *"Do not call to combat."*

Look also at this *hadith* related by Imam al-Saadiq (A) who said:

> *"The Messenger of Allah when he wanted to send out a troop he called them and bid them sit before him. He then said to them: Go out in the name of Allah and by Allah and in the way of Allah and according to the religion of the Messenger of Allah. Do not handcuff or tie up (the prisoners of war), do not mutilate (even the dead), and do not betray people. Do not kill the old man, the child or the woman, and do not cut down a single tree except when you are forced to do so. And if any Muslim be he lofty or lowly gives a man of the Polytheists sanctuary, then his safety must be secured so that he hears the word of Allah. If he follows you then he is your brother in religion. If he refuses then give him his sanctuary and seek the help of Allah regarding him."*

In an account on the occasion of war, Imam *Amir-ul-Mu'mineen* (A) advised the Muslims saying:

> *'Commit yourselves to prayer and guard your prayers and pray much. Seek nearness to Allah through it for it is a duty of the Muslims at prescribed times.'*

He also used to say: *'Do not fight them until they begin to fight you.'*

Islam's Guidance on War

War is something resorted to only in dire emergency, and whether or not it is resorted to come from an evaluation, which in the case of war is particularly important as it involves destruction, annihilation and the termination of life. Hence, Islam has laid down conditions and terms for war despite it having made either offensive or defensive *jihad* obligatory, as is well known in the books of jurisprudence. These many terms and conditions have been laid down so that war only occurs in cases of dire emergency. Then if the war ends, Islam grants a general amnesty and grants the freedom of the wrongdoers wherever possible, as we shall see in the following sections.

The condition of parental permission

Related by Imam Ja'far al-Saadiq (A) who said: *'A man approached the Messenger of Allah (S) and said: 'O Messenger of Allah, I wish to take part in the jihad*[15]*.'* The Messenger of Allah (S) said: *'Then strive in the way of Allah and if you are killed you will find yourself with Allah and be given sustenance*[16]*, and if you die then your reward will be with Allah, and if you return then you will be as free from sin as the day you were born.'* The man said: *'O Messenger of Allah, I have two aged parents who wish that I spend my time in their company and would not like me to go out to battle.'* The Messenger of Allah (S) said: *'Then stay with your parents, for by He in whose hands my soul lies, spending a day and a night in their company is better than one year's jihad."*

Related by Jabir who said: 'A man approached the Messenger of Allah (S) and said: *'I am a strong man and I wish to fight jihad but my mother does not like this.'* The Prophet (S) said: *'Return and be with your mother, for by He who sent me with the truth, you spending one night in her company is better than one year's jihad in the way of Allah.'*

---

[15] Translator's note: The literal meaning of *jihad* is to strive, struggle and exert some effort in some matter. There are two main types of *jihad*. The lesser *jihad* which can be fighting, defending borders, and spreading the rule of Islam (this does not include forced conversions to Islam as these are untenable. It rather means bringing the justice and wisdom of Allah's laws in place of the injustice and fallibility of man made laws.) Then the greater *jihad* as mentioned by the Prophet (S) is that internal struggle to combat the baseness and evil of one's own self.

[16] Translator's note: This is a reference to the Qur'anic verses (3:169) which state that those who are killed while striving in the way of Allah are not to be considered dead but rather alive with their Lord and receiving sustenance.

Ibn 'Abbas relates that the Prophet (S) was approached by a man who said: *'O Messenger of Allah shall I do jihad?'* (Meaning going into battle). The Prophet said: *'Do you have parents?'* The man said: *'Yes.'* So the Prophet said: *'Then do jihad*[17] *for them.'*

Related by Abu Sa'id al-Khudari:

'A man emigrated from Yemen to the Messenger of Allah (S) who said to him: *'Have you anyone in Yemen?'* The man replied that he had two parents there. The Prophet (S) asked: *'Have they given permission to you?'* The man replied: 'No.' The Prophet (S) said: *'Then return and seek their permission and if they give you their permission then fight jihad, and if not then obey them and be kind to them.'*

Jihad is not incumbent upon certain groups

In a *hadith* related by al-Hassan ibn Mahboub, from some of his companions who said:

Imam Muhammad al-Baqir (A) in his letter to one of the Umayyad Caliphs wrote rebuking those Caliphs who had tasked people with things that had not been enjoined by Allah Almighty saying:

> *'. . . the blind and the lame have been wrongly obligated as well as those who do not have the funds to spend on jihad, and this after Allah has granted them exemption.'*

This is according to what is to be found in the Holy Qur'an regarding this matter where the Almighty has said:

> **{Those of the believers who sit (do not go to fight), other than those who have injuries, are not equal to the *mujahidin* who fight in the way of Allah with their wealth and their selves. Allah favours those *mujahidin* who strive in the way of Allah with their wealth and their selves, a degree over those who sit it out. Allah has promised both parties a goodly reward but Allah has favoured those *mujahidin* over those who sit it out with a great reward and by degrees. From Him is a**

[17] Translator's note: The actual wording in Arabic is '*Fa-Jaahid fii himaa.*' (Then 'do *jihad*' for the two of them.') The Prophet (S) here is telling the man that looking after his parents is a kind of *jihad* and a better kind than the kind of *jihad* that involves fighting.'

forgiveness and mercy. Allah is Oft Forgiving Most Merciful.} [18]

{Say to those Bedouin Arabs who lag behind: You will be called to a people of might who you will fight or they will enter Islam. If you obey, then Allah will give you a goodly reward and if you turn away as you turned away before then, Allah will torment you with a painful torment. There is no blame upon the blind man nor upon the cripple nor upon the sick. Whoever obeys Allah and His Messenger will be given entry to gardens below which rivers flow, but whoever turns away will be tormented a painful torment.} [19]

In our book *'al-Fiqh* series: volume 48, *Jihad'* We have mentioned that six groups are exempt from the duty of *jihad*: The blind, the cripple, the sick, the person who cannot cover his expenses, the person to whom *jihad* would be injurious, and the person impeded from *jihad* in general. The duty of *jihad* is not incumbent upon the insane, the slave, or the elderly person.

The Messenger of Allah (S) said: *'The pen[20] is lifted from the youngster until he reaches maturity and from the insane until he regains his mind.'*

Related from Imam 'Ali (A) that he said: *'Jihad is not incumbent upon the slave.'*

There are many other traditions in this regard.

Jihad is not incumbent upon women

Related from al-Asbagh ibn Nabatah who said: '*Amir-ul-Mu'mineen* 'Ali (A) said:

> *'Allah has prescribed jihad for both men and women. The jihad of the man is to spend of his wealth and of his self until he is killed in the way of Allah. The jihad of the woman is to remain patient in the face of problem from her husband."*

In another *hadith*: *'The jihad of the woman is to make a good wife for her husband.'*

---

[18] *The Holy Qur'an*: The Women (4): 95-96.
[19] *The Holy Qur'an*: The Victory (48): 16.
[20] Translators note: the expression the pen is lifted means one would not held accountable for the particular aspect in question.

Related from Imam 'Ali (A) who said:

> *'The duty of jihad does not fall upon the slave when they can be dispensed with, nor upon the woman, nor upon he who has not reached maturity.'*

Also from Imam 'Ali (A) who said:

> *'The Messenger of Allah (S) said: 'Allah has prescribed jihad for the men of my nation (Islam) and jealousy upon the women of my nation. And whoever of the women is patient and seeks a reward, Allah will give her the reward of a martyr.'*

Related by Sayyid 'Ali ibn Tawous who said: 'I saw a *hadith* which said that Wahab was a Christian . . . until it mentioned his death and that his mother entered the battle. Then Imam al-Hussein (A) said to them both: *'Go back O mother of Wahab, you and your son are with the Messenger of Allah (S) for the duty of jihad has been lifted from women.'*

Imam Saadiq (A) was asked about how it came to be that the burden of the *Jizyah* tax has been lifted from women. He (A) said:

> *'Because the Messenger of Allah (S) prohibited the killing of women and children in dar al-harb*[21] *except when they take part in the fighting and even when they take part in the fighting then one should restrain oneself from fighting them as far as is possible. Because this is the case in dar al-harb then this is even more appropriate in dar al-Islam*[22]. *If they were to refuse to pay the Jizyah tax then killing them is not possible and this being the case, then the Jizyah is lifted from them. If the men were to refuse to pay the Jizyah tax then they would be breaking the treaty and therefore killing them would be allowed because the killing of men is allowed in the lands of polytheism. The crippled, the blind, the old man, the women and children of the lands of war are not to be killed and because of this the burden of the Jizyah tax has been lifted from them.*

[21] Meaning 'the land of war', this is a reference to non-Muslim country engaged in a war with the Muslims.
[22] Meaning 'Muslim country'.

War is not permitted in the absence of the just Imam

Related from Yunis who said: 'I was with Imam al-Kaadhem (A) when a man asked the Imam (A): 'One of your followers has heard that a man is giving out swords and bows in the way of Allah so he went to him and took a sword and a bow from him (not knowing the proper way in this matter). He then met some of his companions who told him that this was not allowed and ordered him to return them (the sword and the bow).

Imam al-Kaadhem (A) said: *'Then let him do so.'*

But he replied that he had sought the man but was unable to find him and he was told that the man had died.

Imam al-Kaadhem (A) said: *'Then let him defend but not to fight.'*

The man said: 'and in places like Qazwin, or Ashkelon, or al-Daylam or other citadels?'

Imam al-Kaadhem (A) said: *'Yes.'*

The man said: 'And if the enemy comes to where he is attached, what should he do?'

Imam al-Kaadhem said: *'He should defend the territory of Islam.'*

The man asked: 'Should he fight *jihad*?'

Imam al-Kaadhem (A) said: *'No, unless he fears for the safety of the territory of Islam.'*

The man said: 'Are you saying that if the Romans should enter upon the Muslims, they should not prevent them from doing so.'

Imam al-Kaadhem (A) said: *"He should defend and if he should fear for the safety of Islam and the Muslims then he should fight and his fighting would be for himself (to protect his life, and those of other Muslims) and not for the government (of the time) for if Islam were to be obliterated then the reminder of Muhammad (S) would be obliterated."*

Also related that Imam Saadiq (A) was asked his opinion about a man who entered the land of war safely and then deluded a people who were subject to another people. He (A) said:

> *'The Muslim should defend himself and fight to establish the rule of Allah and His Prophet. It is not allowed that he fight the*

unbelievers under the authority of a tyrannical rule (in a Muslim country) or their traditions.'

Related by Abu 'Urwah al-Sulami, from Imam Saadiq (A) who was asked by a man who said: 'I used to go on frequent military excursions and would travel far in seeking reward and would be absent for long periods of time. This began to be hard on me. Then I was told that there is to be no military campaigns in the absence of the just Imam. What is your opinion?' He (A) said: *'Shall I be brief or in detail?'* He said: 'Why, in detail.' He (A) said: *'Allah will bring the people before him on the Day of Resurrection according to their intentions . . .'* (as if man wished the Imam to be brief.) The man said: 'Tell me in brief.' He (A) said: *'Ask your question.'* The man said: 'If I went on a raid and battled the Polytheists is it necessary to call them to Islam before I fight them?' He (A) said: *'If they raid and fight and are fought then you can fight them. If they are however, a people who have not raided or fought then you may not fight them until you call them to Islam.'*

The man said: 'I called them and one answered and entered Islam in his heart. When he was in the Muslim country, he was treated unjustly, his dignity was violated and his possession was taken from him, and his rights abused. Am I responsible for this, as I had called him to Islam?[23] Imam Saadiq (A) said: *"You are both rewarded for what has happened. It is better that he is with you defending you, your family, your Qiblah and your Book, rather than being against you, fighting you, violating your dignity, spilling your blood and burning book."*

The invitation to Islam . . . firstly

Related by al-Sukuni, from Imam Saadiq (A) who said:

> *'Amir-ul-Mu'mineen 'Ali said: 'The Messenger of Allah sent me to Yemen and said: 'O 'Ali, do not fight anyone until you have invited him to Islam for if Allah should give his guidance to one man through your hands it would be better for you than the whole Earth and you would have his loyalty O 'Ali.'*

Related in the book *Da'aim al-Islam* from Imam 'Ali (A) who said: *'A people should not be fought until they have been invited to Islam.'*

---

[23] It should be noted that save the first Imam, Imam Ali (A), all other imams did not officially assume the office of government. Instead the Muslim were governed tyrants and despots . . .

If the call to Islam has not reached them then you may not fight them, and if even they have been invited to Islam before, to reconfirm the invitation once more is even better.

Related in the book *Ghawali al-Layali* from the Prophet (S) who said: *'The infidels should not be fought until after the invitation to Islam.'*

Also from the book *Da'aim al-Islam*: Related from Imam al-Saadiq (A), from his forefathers, from Amir-ul-Mu'mineen (A) that whenever the Messenger of Allah (S) sent an army or a raiding party, would enjoin God fearing piety upon its leader personally and then upon the rest of the troops in general and would say: *'Fight in the name of Allah and in the way of Allah and according to the creed of the Messenger of Allah (S). Do not fight the people until you have the justification by inviting them to testify that there is no god but Allah and that Muhammad is his messenger and to confirm what he (Muhammad) has brought from Allah. If they respond then they are your brothers in faith and you should then invite them to move from their territory to the towns of the Muslims . . .'* (This is so that they can learn more about Islam in Muslim populated cities where there are centres of learning of Islamic sciences.)

Limiting (fighting) to the least amount necessary

Related by Imam Saadiq (A) who said:

> *"The Messenger of Allah (S), when he wanted to send a troop, he would summon them and bid them sit by him. Then he would say: 'Go in the name of Allah and in the way of Allah and according to the creed of the Messenger of Allah. Do not handcuff or tie up (prisoners) and do not mutilate (even the dead) and do not use treacherous means and do not kill old men or children women. Do not cut down trees unless you are forced to do so. If any Muslim man be he lowly or lofty should look towards one of the Polytheists then he should be given sanctuary so that he might hear the words of Allah. If he follows you then he is your brother in faith and if he refuses then grant him sanctuary and seek succour in Allah."*

Also related from Imam Saadiq (A) who said:

> *"When the Prophet (S) assigned a leader to an expedition squadron, he would enjoin upon him God fearing piety for his*

own person and for his companions generally. He would then say: 'Fight in the name of Allah and in the way of Allah. Fight those who disbelieve in Allah. Do not use treacherous means, do not plunder and do not mutilate. Do not kill children or hermits and do not set fire to date palms or drown them with water. Do not cut down a fruit-bearing tree and do not burn crops for you never know when you might be in need of them. Do not slay animals whose meat is edible except what is necessary for you to eat.

If you should meet an enemy to the Muslims then invite them to one of three things. If they respond to you accordingly then accept them and refrain from any action. Call them to Islam and if they enter Islam then accept them and refrain from any action. Having accepted Islam, then invite them to emigrate to the lands of Islam[24] *and if they do this then accept them and refrain from any action. If they refuse to emigrate and favour their own homes and refuse to enter into the land of the hijra (i.e. the land of Muslim emigrant) then they will have the station of the Bedouin Muslims and have the same rights afforded to them as the Bedouin Muslims. They will not have rights of a share of booty until they emigrate in the way of Allah. If they refuse these two things then call them to pay the Jizyah from their wealth and in a state of humiliation (to contribute to their protection by the Islamic state). If they pay the Jizyah then accept it from them and refrain from any action. If they refuse then seek succour from Allah Almighty against them and fight them in the way of Allah to the utmost.*

If you lay siege to a fortress and the people therein wish you to let them surrender on the basis of the rule of Allah then do not accept that. But rather let them surrender according to your terms and condition, then judge what you will regarding them according to the criteria you know best. For if you let them surrender according to the rule of Allah you will not know whether you will be able to fulfil the rule of Allah regarding them or not. If you lay siege to a fortress and the people wish you to let them surrender on the basis of the covenant and assurance of Allah then do not agree to this. Rather let them surrender on the basis of your own covenant and guarantee and that of your

[24] This is in order to for them to be close centres of Islamic learning and therefore learn more about Islam in the various domains of life.

fathers and your brothers. For if you break your covenant and the covenant of your fathers and your brothers it will be easier for you on the Day of Resurrection than if you had broken the covenant of Allah and His messenger."

Related from Imam Saadiq (A) from his father, from his forefathers, from Amir-ul-Mu'mineen (A) who said:

> *"The Messenger of Allah (S), when he sent out an army or a raiding party would enjoin God fearing piety upon its leader personally and on the rest of the Muslims who were with him. He (S) would say: 'Fight in the name of Allah and in the way of Allah . . . and do not kill children or the elderly or women (meaning as long as they do not fight you), and do not mutilate and do not tie up or handcuff, and do not use perfidious means."*

Related by al-Sukuni, from Imam Saadiq (A) who said:

> *'Amir-ul-Mu'mineen (A) said: 'The Messenger of Allah (S) forbade the letting loose or deploying of poison in the lands of the Polytheists.'*

Related from Ja'far ibn Muhammad, from his father, from his grandfather 'Ali ibn al-Hussein, from his father from Imam 'Ali (A) who said:

> *'The Messenger of Allah (S) said: 'In battle do not kill (anyone) except those who have exposed themselves to the blades. (i.e. those who have come to fight with you.)*

Related in the book *Da'aim al-Islam* that the Messenger of Allah (S) said: *'Do not kill children or the elderly or women.'*

Related in a *hadith* is that Sa'd ibn Mu'adh judged regarding the clan of Qureidah "that their fighters be killed and that their children be captured. He ordered that the male amongst the captured to have their garments removed. Whoever's had grown was considered to be a fighter and whoever's had not grown then he was considered to be one of the children"[25]. The Prophet (S) accepted this.

[25] The clan of Qureidah had signed a binding agreement with the Muslims that they be allowed to stay in Madinah and have the protection of the Muslims, on the condition that they would not aid the enemies of the Muslims, the Polytheists, against the Muslims. This came about after a number of aggressions and assaults by the clan against the Muslims directly, as well as aiding their enemies against them. In the year 5 Hijra (after the Prophet's migration from Mecca to Madinah), all the different Polytheist groups and clans

No war when sanctuary is given

Related from Imam Saadiq (A) who was asked: 'What is the meaning of the Prophet's saying: *'The lowliest of them strives for their protectorate.'*

He (A) answered: *"If a Muslim army were to lay siege to a group of Polytheists and a man looked out from the fortress and said: 'Give me sanctuary so that I may meet your leader and discuss with him.' If then the lowliest of the Muslims gives the pledge of sanctuary then it is binding also upon the most high-ranking of them."*

Related from Imam Saadiq (A) who said:

> *'If a group laid siege to a city and the people ask for sanctuary but they are told 'No', but they thought that they have been told 'Yes' and come down to them then they have sanctuary.'*

Amir-ul-Mu'mineen (A) said:

> *'If someone promises another a truce on his blood then betrays that truce then I disassociate myself from the killer even though the one killed may be destined for the fire.'*

In the covenant of Amir-ul-Mu'mineen, Imam 'Ali (A), to al-Ashtar (May Allah have mercy upon him) states:

> *"Do not reject outright a truce called for by your enemy and in it is the pleasure of Allah. For the truce is an occasion of respite for*

---

started to mobilise their forces against the Muslims in order to finish them off, once and for all. The subsequent battle that took place between the confederation of the various clans and the Polytheist groups, and the Muslims became known as the Battle of al-Ahzab (the Confederates). Leading up to the battle, and after seeing the size of the mobilised forces against the Muslims, the Qureidah clan considered it to be a good opportunity to join ranks with the confederates against the Muslims, in order to succeed in obliterating them. Therefore the elders and warriors of the clan decided to break the agreement they had signed with the Muslims and side with Polytheists against them. According to the agreement, this act in itself constituted a declaration of war by the Qureidah clan against the Muslims. At the end of the day, the Muslims were the victors of the Battle of al-Ahzab.

According to the agreement, the Muslims had the right to wage war against the Qureidah clan, but instead asked the Qureidah clan for their suggestion as to how to settle this matter. They proposed that a third party judges this matter and his judgment would be final. The Muslims asked the Qureidah clan to propose a candidate that might be acceptable to both sides. The Qureidah clan proposed Sa'd ibn Mu'adh, the Muslims accepted the proposed candidate. Sa'd ibn Mu'adh was known to be have been a long time friend of the Qureidah clan, and he was known to have accepted Islam. He was then invited by both sides to make judgment on the matter, according to the agreement between the two parties. He accepted and made the above judgement.

your troops and a rest for you from your worries and concerns and a security for your lands. But remember be on your guard to the utmost after making a truce, for it may be that the enemy seeks to draw close to you in order to take you unawares. Therefore be judicious and do not give them the benefit of the doubt.

If you should form a treaty between you and your enemy which gives him your protectorate and word of honour, then honour this treaty, proclaim your word of honour and make yourself as a shield guarding what you have given, for there is no commandment of Allah (Almighty is He) more acknowledged in the eyes of the people despite the difference of their ideas and opinions than the honouring of pledges. Even the Polytheists have practised this amongst themselves because they realise the evil consequences of treachery. Do not betray your covenant and do not break your contract and do not double cross your enemy for Allah has made His covenant and protectorate a sanctuary for his servants through His mercy and none but the ignorant wretch would go against Allah in this way. Therefore there should be no interpolation, forgery or betrayal in this matter. Do not formulate a treaty in which there is room for ambiguity. When the treaty has been ratified and concluded do not try to take advantage of any grammatical errors that may be in it.

Do not let a critical situation arising from the treaty of Allah cause you to rescind it without just cause, for your patience in this situation seeking relief from it and the best outcome is better than treachery the dire consequences of which you fear and that you will be overcome by, and liable to that (treachery) and therefore be called upon by Allah to account for it and hence you will not be able to seek forgiveness for it in this world or in the hereafter."

Related from Imam 'Ali (A) who said:

'The Messenger of Allah (S) gave a sermon in the mosque of al-Hanif saying: 'May Allah have mercy on the person who hears this speech and remembers it and then passes it on to one who has not heard it. For many a person who bears knowledge is not a scholar but may transmit that knowledge to one more knowledgeable than him. The heart of the Muslim will never cheat after the knowledge of three things: Dedicating one's

> *actions to Allah only, giving good counsel to the leaders of the Muslims, and being bound to the fact that the Muslims are a brotherhood. For with unity, the call of the Muslims will be overwhelming (on the non-Muslims). The blood of Muslims is equal, the lowliest of them may offer their protectorate, for if any of the Muslims should give sanctuary to any of the heathens then this is binding.'*

Also related from Amir-ul-Mu'mineen 'Ali (A) who said:

> *'If a Muslim should make a gesture of truce or sanctuary to any of the Polytheists and he descends (from a fortress) accordingly then he has the truce.'*

Related from Imam Saadiq (A) who said: *'Truce is allowed in whatever language it may be in.'*

Related from Amir-ul-Mu'mineen 'Ali (A) who said: *'Fulfil your promises if you make a promise.'*

He (A) also said: *'If any Muslim makes a gesture of truce to any of the enemy then he has a truce.'*

Related from Imam Saadiq (A) who was asked about two towns in enemy territory each with their own king. These towns fight one another and then make peace. Then one of the kings betrays the other and comes to the Muslims and makes a truce with them on the condition that they raid the other city. Imam Saadiq (A) said:

> *'It is not fitting for the Muslims to use treachery or to order others to be treacherous, nor to fight alongside those who are treacherous. They should fight the Polytheists whenever possible (according to the specified conditions), provided there are no binding peace treaties between them and the Infidels.'*

Also related from Imam Saadiq (A) who said: *The Messenger of Allah (S) said: 'Each traitor will come on the Day of Judgement mouth-twisted until he enters the fire."*

Related by al-Asbagh ibn Nabatah who said: 'Amir-ul-Mu'mineen (A) one day when he was giving a sermon on the pulpit of Kufa said:

> *'O people. Were it not for the vileness of treachery, you would find me to be the craftiest of people. But with each act of treason there is an depraved act and with each depraved act there is an*

> *act of infidelity and indeed treason, depravity, and betrayal are for the fire.'*

Related from Imam 'Ali (A) that the Messenger of Allah (S) said regarding a treaty of his:

> *'Beware of breaking the treaty of Allah and His protectorate. For Allah has made His treaty and protectorate a sanctuary for all His servants by His mercy. Having patience in a time of strife in which you seek relief is better than any treachery in which you fear its repercussions and evil consequences.'*

Amir-ul-Mu'mineen 'Ali (A) said in a *hadith*:

> *'The fulfilment of promises is a concomitant of sincerity and I do not know of a shield more efficient than it (fulfilment). No one who is aware of the return (to Allah) would ever commit treachery. But we now live in a time when most of the people have taken up treachery as the clever and crafty way of conduct. The ignorant people would attribute this as a good conduct. What is the matter with them? May Allah curse them. The truly intelligent one knows the ways and has the means to attain whatever he wishes, but the thing that prevents him from doing so, is the order of Allah. He refrains from committing (anything which is against the pleasure of Allah) even though he is able to do it. Whereas the one who has no fear of Allah or no bound to religion would not loose the opportunity to grab it."*

He (A) also said: *'Fulfilling promises to the people of treachery is treachery in the sight of Allah. Likewise treachery towards the people of treachery is as the fulfilment of promises in the sight of Allah.'*

Author's note: Here Imam 'Ali (A) alludes to the principle of degrees of importance, and the meaning here is not treachery but rather that the command of Allah is more important than being trustworthy towards the treacherous by excusing oneself from being on the side of the treacherous for one's own protection.

Related from the Prophet (S) who said:

> *There are four things which if found in a person then he is a hypocrite . . . (and one of them is that) if he makes a promise he breaks it.'*

Related from Amir-ul-Mu'mineen 'Ali (A) who said:

'The swiftest of things in their consequences is when you make a contract with a person and you intend to keep it but he intends to break it.'

Cease fire during the Sacred Months

Related from 'Ala' ibn al-Fudail who said: 'I asked him Imam Saadiq (A) about whether the Muslims should initiate fighting with the Polytheists during the Sacred Months. He (A) said:

> *'If the Polytheists initiate things by considering fighting allowed during these months and the Muslims see that they are being vanquished then they should fight and this because of Allah Almighty's words:* **{The Sacred Month for the Sacred Month and the law of equality applies for the sacred things}.** [26]

The Romans were in this regard in the same position as that of the Polytheists because they did not recognise sanctity for the Sacred Months and would initiate fighting during these months. The Polytheists did however know about the sanctity of the Sacred Months but they considered fighting to be allowed as did the unjust who used to initiate fighting.

Related from 'Ali ibn Ibrahim in his exegesis: 'The Sacred Months are the months of *Rajab* on its own and then *Dhul-Qa'dah, Dhul-Hijjah,* and *Muharram* consecutively in which Allah has prohibited fighting and the effects of sins are multiplied and also good deeds.'

Prisoners of war are not to be killed

Related from al-Zuhri, from Imam 'Ali ibn al-Hussein (A) who said (in a *hadith*):

> *'If you take a prisoner and he is incapable of walking and you do not have a carriage then send him on his way (set him free) and do not kill him for you do not know what the Imam will rule regarding him.'*

He also said:

> *'The prisoner, if he enters Islam will be spared his life and he will become part of the group.'*

---

[26] *The Holy Qur'an*: The Heifer (2): 194.

Related from 'Abdullah ibn Maymoun who said: "Imam 'Ali (A) was brought a prisoner on the day of the battle of Siffin and the prisoner pledged allegiance to him. Imam 'Ali (A) said:

> *'I will not kill you for I fear Allah Lord of the worlds.' So he sent him on his way and returned to him the booty that he had come with.'*

Related from Amir-ul-Mu'mineen Imam 'Ali (A) who said:

> *"The Messenger of Allah (S) took some prisoners on the day of the battle of Badr and took ransom in exchange for their freedom.* (similarly there were exchanges of prisoners of war.) *For the Imam has the choice, if Allah grants him victory over the Polytheists, to kill the warriors from them or to take them as prisoners and count them amongst the spoils of war and to divide them up. And if the Imam see it to be in the general interest, he could set them free."*

Related from Bashir, who said to Imam Saadiq (A): 'I had a dream in which I said to you: 'Fighting without an Imam to whom obedience is mandatory is prohibited in the same way that eating the flesh of animals not slaughtered (according to the Islamic law), or blood, or swine flesh is prohibited.' Then you said to me (in the dream): 'Yes, this is the case.' Imam Saadiq (A) said: *'Yes this is indeed the case.'*

Related from Sama'ah, from Imam Saadiq (A) who said: 'Abbad al-Basri met Ali ibn al-Hussein (A) on the road to Makkah and said to him: 'O Ali son of al-Hussein, you have left *jihad* and its difficulties and turned to the Hajj and its easiness for indeed Allah Almighty and Exalted is He has said:

> **{Surely Allah has bought from the Believers their own selves and their wealth in return for Paradise, that they fight in the way of Allah . . .}**[27]

Ali ibn al-Hussein (A) said: *'Read on.'* He said: **{Those who turn in repentance and do acts of worship . . .}**[28]

Then Ali ibn al-Hussein (A) said:

> *"If we see those people who are described thus, then jihad with them is better then the Hajj."*

---

[27] *The Holy Qur'an*: Repentance (9): 111.

[28] *The Holy Qur'an*: Repentance (9): 112.

Related from Muhammad ibn 'Abdullah al-Samandari who said: 'I said to Imam Saadiq (A): 'If I was by the gate (meaning the main gate) and there was a call to arms should I go with them?'

He (A) said:

> *"Do you think that if you went out with them and you took a man prisoner then granted him sanctuary and gave him the same treaty that the Messenger of Allah (S) used to give to the Polytheists, would they fulfil the covenant?"*

I said: 'No they would not fulfil it.'

He (A) said: *"Then do not go out with them."*

Related form Abu Basir, from Imam Saadiq (A), from his forefathers (A) who said:

> *"The Muslim should not go out for jihad if he does not safeguard the rule or implement the command of Allah Almighty. If he were to die in that place he would be an aide to our enemy in limiting our right and putting our blood in danger. His death would be a death as of the days of ignorance.'*

Related from Ja'far ibn Muhammad (A) in the *hadith* of the *sharai'a al-din* who said: *'Jihad is mandatory with the just Imam, and whoever is killed defending his wealth is a martyr.'*

Related from Bashshara al-Mustapha, from Komeil, from Amir-ul-Mu'mineen 'Ali (A) who said: *'O Komeil, there is to be no military raids without a just Imam.'*

Related from Sayyid 'Ali ibn Tawous in the book *Kashf al-Yaqin* with the chain of narration to the Prophet (S) regarding the blessed night ascension to Heaven: Allah Almighty revealed to the Prophet (S): *'Walking on foot to jihad is only with you or with the Imams from your progeny.'*

Related from al-Sha'bi who said: 'When Imam 'Ali (A) took prisoners on the day of Siffin he set them free. 'Amr ibn al-'Aas had said (to Mu'awiyah): "Kill the prisoners you have taken." In the mean time the freed prisoners started to arrive at Mu'awiyah's camp. Mu'awiyah then said to 'Amr ibn al-'Aas: 'O 'Amr, if we were to follow what you say then we would indeed fall into a foul state of affairs and our reputation would be worsened. Do you not see that our prisoners have been released? Then he ordered that the prisoners from Imam 'Ali's men be released. When Imam Ali (a) had taken a prisoner from the Syrian camp, he would released him except when one of his own men had been killed in which case he would kill him for that. Also if Imam Ali (A) released a prisoner and he returned once more to fight, he would kill him then.

Author's note: The killing of the prisoners was only in extraordinary cases because the Imam release of prisoners is well recorded in the chronicles. The account of Asbagh ibn Darar, presented later, is one example of this.

Those who were forced to fight should not be killed

In the book *Da'aim al-Islam*, related from Amir-ul-Mu'mineen 'Ali (A) who said:

> *'The Messenger of Allah (S) said on the day of the battle of Badr: 'Whoever you capture of the Clan of 'Abd al-Muttalib, then do not kill them for they have been forced to fight against their wills.'*

Tolerance in the treatment of the enemy

Related from Hafs ibn Ghayyath, who said: 'I asked Imam Saadiq (A) about the case of two groups of Believers, one of them unjust and the other just. What if the unjust were to defeat the just in battle?'

He (A) replied: *'It is not the way of those who are just to pursue one retreating or to kill prisoners, or to finish off the wounded . . .'*

Related in a *hadith* from Abu Hamzah al-Thumali, from Imam 'Ali ibn al-Hussein (A) who said:

> *'Imam Ali (A) wrote to Malik, who was in the avant-guard on the day of al-Basrah (the Battle of Jamal), that he was only to lance those who were charging and he was not to kill men who were retreating or to kill the wounded and whoever bolts his door will be safe.*

Related from 'Abdullah ibn Sharik, from his father who said: 'When the people were defeated on the day of the battle of the Camel (*Jamal*), Amir-ul-Mu'mineen (A) said: *'Do not pursue one retreating and do not kill the wounded and whoever bolts his door will be spared.'*

Related from Imam Ridha (A) that

> *"Imam 'Ali (A) on the day of the battle of the Jamal did not pursue anyone retreating, nor did he finish off the wounded, and anyone who threw down his weapons would be spared as would anyone who entered his own house."*

In one account it is said:

> *"If the unjust were defeated and they had a troop and a base which they could resort to, they would be sought and their wounded finished off, and they would be pursued and killed as far as possible*[29]*. Amir-ul-Mu'mineen (A) did the same with the people of Siffin because Mu'awiya was behind them. If they had not had a troop to return to, they would not be sought and their wounded would not be finished off, because if they retreated they would split up and scatter."*

We have also related that

> *"During the battle of the Jamal when Talhah and al-Zubeir were killed and 'Aishah was arrested and the People of the Jamal were defeated, the order was proclaimed by the herald of Amir-ul-Mu'mineen (A): 'Do not kill the wounded, do not pursue anyone retreating and whoever throws down his weapon will be spared."*
>
> *Then Amir-ul-Mu'mineen (A) called for the mule of the Prophet (S), which he mounted. Then he said 'Come you, and Come you until he had gathered around him almost sixty elders all of them from the Hamdan (tribe) who had taken up sword, shield and helm. Then he went with them still around him until they reached a magnificent house where he asked to be admitted and he was admitted.*
>
> *He then found himself amongst a group of women all bewailing in the courtyard of the house, and when they saw him they began to shriek and say: 'He is the killer of our beloveds.' However he did not say anything to them. He asked the whereabouts of the chamber of 'Aishah. The door was opened and he was admitted. Then it was heard that in their conversation 'Aishah was apologetic – "No by Allah", "Yes by Allah". Then he exited and looked towards a woman and said: 'Come here O Saffiyah.' She hurried towards him and he said to her: 'Do you not dismiss*

---

[29] This is because they could regroup and reinforce and come back again.

those who say that I am the killer of beloveds. For if I was the killer of beloveds I would have killed those who are in that chamber, and in this one, and in this one.' He indicated three rooms. The woman went to the other women and those in the house who were wailing fell silent and those standing sat down.'

Al-Asbagh (The narrator of the hadith) said: 'In one of the rooms was 'Aishah[30] *and her confidantes. In another room were Marwan ibn al Hakam and some young men of the Qureish. In another were 'Abdullah ibn al-Zubeir and his folk.' Al-Asbagh was asked: 'So why did you not raise your hands against those people. Were they not the cause of the sore? Why did you let them live?' He said: 'We took hold of our swords and narrowed our eyes towards Imam 'Ali (A) waiting for his command to kill them but he did not do so and instead chose to grant a general amnesty."*

Sheikh al-Mufid has said in the book *"al-Kafi'a fi Ibtal taubat al-Khati'a"*, from Abu Mukhnaf Lut ibn Yahya, from 'Abdullah ibn 'Asim, from Muhammad ibn Bashir al-Hamdani who said: 'The letter of Amir-ul-Mu'mineen (A) came with 'Umar ibn Salma al-Awha to the People of Kufa. He saluted the people so that all the people could hear it and gathered in the Mosque. The call to congregational prayer was announced and not one person tarried. Then the letter was read:

> *'In the Name of Allah The Beneficent The Merciful. From 'Abdullah Amir-ul-Mu'mineen (A) to Qarzah ibn Ka'b and the Muslims; Peace be upon you, I praise Allah there is no deity but He. Now, we have met with the treacherous people . . . (until he said) and when Allah had defeated them, I ordered that no-one retreating should be pursued, nor should the wounded be killed, nor should the nakedness of anyone be exposed nor clothing torn. No house should be entered without permission and the people have safety."*

Related from Habba al-'Arani in a *hadith* saying: 'On the day of the Jamal, the people came out to face each other . . . (until he relates) the (rebellious) people retreated defeated then the herald of Amir-ul-Mu'mineen (A) called that *"the wounded were not to be killed, those retreating were not to be pursued, that whoever locks his door will be spared and whoever throws down his weapon will be spared."*

---

[30] 'Aishah instigated and led the Battle (of Jamal) against Imam 'Ali (A).

Related from Muhammad al-Hanafiyyah son of Imam 'Ali (A) who said: 'I had the standard (flag) on the day of the Jamal . . . (until he said) then he ordered his herald to proclaim that: *'No wounded person should be attacked, nor should any retreating person be pursued. Whoever locks his door will be safe.'*

It is related that amongst the people of al-Sham (The army of Mu'awiya from Damascus) was a man named al-Asbagh ibn Darar and that he formed an armed vanguard. Imam 'Ali charged al-Ashtar with him and he took him prisoner without a fight. Imam 'Ali (A) used to forbid the killing of prisoners. Al-Ashtar came with him at night and made fast his bonds and put him with his guests to await the morning. This man al-Asbagh was an eloquent poet and he felt sure that he would be killed while his companions slept. So he raised his voice and let al-Ashtar hear some verses of poetry describing his condition and seeking to evoke his emotions.

In the morning al-Ashtar came to Imam 'Ali (A) and said: 'O Commander of The Faithful! This is a man from the army who I met yesterday. By Allah if I knew it was right to kill him I would kill him. He spent the night with us last night and moved us. If it is to be that we kill him then I will kill him. If we are angry at him or we have a choice then give him to me. Imam 'Ali (A) said: *'He is yours O Malik. For if you take a prisoner from the people-of-the-Kiblah (i.e. Muslims) you should not kill him. The prisoners from the people of the Kiblah are neither ransomed nor killed.'* So al-Ashtar returned with him to his house and said: 'Yours is what we took from you and nothing more than that.'

Related from Salam who said: 'I witnessed the battle of the Jamal . . . (until he said) When the people of Basrah were defeated, the herald of Imam 'Ali (A) proclaimed:

> *'Do not pursue those retreating, nor one who throws down his weapon, and do not kill the wounded. For these people are retreating and they have no troop to resort to. This is what the Sunnah commended when fighting the trespassers."*

In the book *Da'aim al-Islam,* relating that Imam 'Ali (A) was asked by 'Ammar when he entered Basrah: 'O Commander of the Believers! How shall we treat these people? He (A) answered: *'With open-handedness and kindness just as the Prophet (S) did with the people of Makkah."*

Related from Musa ibn Talha ibn 'Ubeidullah (who was amongst those taken prisoner on the day of the Jamal) who said: 'I was in the prison of 'Ali (A) in Basrah when I heard a herald calling: 'Where is Musa son of Talha son of 'Ubeidullah?

'I invoked the words: 'Verily we belong to Allah and verily we shall to him return.' This also did the people of the prison saying: 'He will kill you.'

They brought me out and when I was in front of him he said to me: *'O Musa!'*

I said: 'At your service O Commander of the Faithful.'

He said: *'Say 'I seek the forgiveness of Allah'.*

I said: 'I seek the forgiveness of Allah and I turn towards Him in repentance' three times.' He said to his messengers: *'Release him.'* Then he said to me: *'Go wherever you wish and whatever you find among our soldiers in the way of arms then take them and fear Allah in the future and sit in your house.'*

So I expressed my gratitude and left. The companions of Imam 'Ali (A) had taken as spoils what the opposing army had brought to the battle to fight him with (i.e. weapons), but nothing other than that.'

Related from 'Abdullah ibn Ja'far al-Humeiri, with a chain of narration from Ja'far al-Saadiq (A), from his father (A) that

> *Imam 'Ali (A) did not attribute the crime of shirk*[31] *to anyone he made war with nor that of hypocrisy, but he used to say: 'They are our brothers who have trespassed against us.'*

Justification to the enemy, and not initiating attack

Related from al-'Ayyashi, with a chain of narration from Imam Saadiq (A) that Imam 'Ali (A) said to his companions on the day of Basrah: *'Do not hastily attack them until we have a justification in the sight of Allah Almighty and them.'* He stood up and addressed the people of Basrah saying: *'Do you find any injustice from me in my ruling?'* They said: 'No.'

---

[31] . . . in general polytheism or ascribing partners to Allah.

In the book *Da'aim al-Islam*, of Amir-ul-Mu'mineen 'Ali (A) who gave a sermon in Kufah when a man from the Kharijites stood up and said: 'There is no rule except that of Allah.' Amir-ul-Mu'mineen fell silent. Then another stood up and another and another and when their number became great he (A) said:

> *'This is a word of truth but its objective is falsehood. With us, you have three rights: we would not prevent you from praying in the Mosques of Allah, nor would we prevent you from spoils of war as long as your hands are with our hands (i.e. you take part in war along side us), and we would not initiate war against you until you initiate it.'*

Related from 'Abdullah ibn Jondab, from his father that Amir-ul-Mu'mineen 'Ali (A) used to give orders about every land in which we found the enemy saying:

> *'Do not fight the people until they initiate fighting for then by the grace of Allah you will have the justification, and leaving them until they initiate fighting is yet another justification. Then if you defeat them, do not kill one who is fleeing, and do not finish off the wounded or expose nakedness or mutilate the dead.'*

Al-Kulaini said in another speech of Imam 'Ali's (A): 'If you meet those people tomorrow, then do not fight them until they fight you, but if they start on you then fall upon them.'

Sheikh al-Mufid has related in The Book of *Irshad* in the context of the death of Imam al-Hussein (A) and his arrival at Nineveh saying: Zuheir ibn al-Qayn said to al-Hussein (A): 'By Allah, I can only believe that after those who you see now (i.e. Hurr and his army) will come a force stronger than those you see. O Son of the Messenger of Allah! To fight them now would be easier than to fight those who come after them. Upon my life, we will not be able to kill those who will come after them .'

Al-Hussein (A) said: ***'It is not for me to begin the fighting.'*** Then he dismounted.

(The *hadith* continues and gives an account of the day of 'Ashura).

Then, on the day of 'Ashura, Shimr ibn Dhil-Jawshan (May the curse of Allah be upon him) called at the top of his voice: 'O Hussein, Do you seek the fire before the Day of Resurrection?'

Al-Hussein (A) said: *'Who is this? It seems like Shimr Son of Dhil-Jawshan.'*

They said : 'Yes it is.'

He (A) said: *'O Son of a Goatherd, you are more worthy of (being cast into) the fire!'*

Then Muslim ibn 'Ausijah made to fire an arrow at him but al-Hussein (A) prevented him. He said let me shoot him for he is a criminal and enemy of Allah and great tyrant.'

Al-Hussein (A) said to him: *'No, do not shoot him for I would hate to begin the fighting against them.'*

Women not to be harmed

The book *al-Kafi* of Kuleini relates in the *hadith* of Malik ibn A'yun, from Amir-ul-Mu'mineen (A) that he said:

> *'Do not mutilate the dead, and if you reach the caravan of the people then do not tear any veils. Do not enter any houses and do not take anything of their belongings except that which you find in their military camp. Do not harm any women even if they insult your honour or curse your leaders and notables for they are weaker in physical strength, numbers and intellect. We have been ordered not to harm them even if they are Polytheists and if a man was to harm a woman he will be rebuked for it and he will suffer the consequences."*

Author's note: In the beginning of the Book of Marriage in *Sharh al-'Urwah* we have dealt with Imam 'Ali's saying that women are lacking in intellect, share of wealth and faith.

Messengers not to be killed

'Abd Allah ibn Ja'far al-Humeiri, from Ja'far al-Saadiq (A), from his father (A), from his forefathers (A), from the Messenger of Allah (S) who said: *'The messenger is not to be killed.'*

In the book *Da'aim al-Islam*, related from Amir-ul-Mu'mineen (A) who said: *'If you capture a man from your enemy and he claims that he is a messenger sent to you then if he brings proof supporting his claim then you have no way against him until he delivers the message and returns to his companions. However if you do not find any proof of his claim then it will not be accepted from him.'*

Prohibition of fighting not in accordance with the Sunnah

Related from Zayd ibn 'Ali, from his forefathers (A) who said: *'The Messenger of Allah (S) said: 'If two Muslims meet with their swords not in accordance with the Sunnah, then both the killer and the one killed will be in the fire.'* He was asked: 'O Messenger of Allah We understand about the killer but why the one killed also?' He (S) said: *'Because he wanted to fight.'*

In the book *Da'aim al-Islam*, related from Imam 'Ali (A) that the Messenger of Allah (S) said to him: *'Woe betide you if you make haste to spill blood illicitly, for there is nothing worse in consequences than this.'*

Cowards are not to go to war

The Ja'faris relate with a chain of narration going back to the Messenger of Allah (S) that he said: 'He who feels in himself cowardice then he should not do battle.'

The Covenanter (Dhimmi) not to be killed

Ja'far ibn Muhammad al-Qummi relates from al-Muttalib that the Prophet (S) said:

> *'He who kills a man from the People of the Dhimma*[32] *will be forbidden Paradise the perfume of which can be smelled at a distance of twelve years travelling.'*

The noblemen of the Infidels to be respected

Muhammad ibn Jarir al-Tabarri relates: 'When the Persian prisoners reached al-Madinah, 'Umar ibn al-Khattab wanted to sell the women, and to enslave the men, but Amir-ul-Mu'mineen (A) said: *'The Messenger of Allah (S) said: 'Honour the nobles of every people.'*

---

[32] People of the Dhimma are the non-Muslims who live under the protection of an Islamic system of government.

'Umar said: 'I heard him saying: *'If a nobleman of a people comes to you then honour him even if he goes against you.'*

Amir-ul-Mu'mineen (A) said:

> *'These people have made peace with you and wish to enter Islam and they are bound to have children. Hence I testify to Allah and to you that I have set free my share of them for the sake of Allah.'*

The Muhajiroun and the Ansar said: 'We give up our right to you O Brother of the Messenger of Allah (S).

He (A) said: *'Allah, I testify that they have given up to me their right and I have accepted it and I testify to You that I have set them free for Your sake.'*

Then 'Umar said: 'Why did you contradict my decision regarding the Persians?, and what was it that made you go against my opinion regarding them.?'

Then Imam 'Ali (A) repeated for him what the Messenger of Allah had said regarding the honouring of nobles.'

Then 'Umar said: 'I give up to Allah and to you O Abu al-Hassan my share and the rest of that which has not been given to you.'

Then Amir-ul-Mu'mineen said: *'O Allah, I testify to what he has said and the responsibility is now upon my head.'*

But a group of the Qureish wanted to marry the women. Amir-ul-Mu'mineen (A) said: *'They are not to be forced to do this but let them have the choice in the matter and what they choose let it be done . . .'*

Not taking booty is a desirable act

'Ali ibn Asbat relates, from Ibn Faddal, from Ja'far al-Saadiq (A), from his father (A), from his forefathers (A), that *Imam 'Ali (A) used to partake in the fighting himself but did not use to take booty."*

Children are not to be killed

This can be found in the account of when the Messenger of Allah ratified the ruling of Sa'd who had ordered that those amongst the Jews who had not reached maturity should not be killed.

Trees are not to be felled, nor the supply of water cut off

It is related from the Messenger of Allah (S) that he *forbade the cutting down or burning of fruiting trees in enemy territory and elsewhere except when this might be to the advantage of the Muslims.* For Allah Almighty has said:

> **{ . . . and what you cut of the date palms or what you leave standing on their trunks is by the leave of Allah and to punish the evildoers}.** [33]

It is also reported that during the battle of Khaibar, the Messenger of Allah (S) was shown by a certain Jew a water source that flowed towards the Khaibar fortress. The Jew said to the Prophet (S): 'If you cut off this water supply then those inside the fortress will surely surrender.' The Messenger of Allah (S) said: *'I will not do this.'* He did not cut the water supply off from them. Nor did Imam 'Ali (A) cut off the water supply from the company of Mu'awiya.

---

[33] *The Holy Qur'an*: Banishment (59):5.

Islam's View on Killing

Islam only sanctions killing in the most grave degree of necessity. Hence it takes a very serious view of the killing of people unjustly. What follows is an overview of some texts relating to this subject.

Islam takes a serious view of the unjust killing of people

Imam Muhammad al-Baqir (A) was asked about Allah's words:

> **{ . . . Whosoever kills a person except for the murder of another or because of spreading corruption in the land, it is as if he has killed the people in their entirety.}**[34]

He said:

> *'He will have a seat in the fire. If he has killed all the people then he will only get that seat.'*

Author's note: It is clear that his torment will be worse as will be mentioned later. This is because the killing of even a single person is not a small matter.

Related from Hamran who said: 'I asked Muhammad al-Baqir (A) about Allah's words:

> **{. . . and because of this We prescribed for the Sons of Israel that whoever kills a person except for the murder of another or for spreading corruption in the land, it is as if he has killed the people in their entirety.}**[35]

I said: 'How is it as if he has killed the people in their entirety when he may only have killed one?'

He (A) said: *'He will be put into a place in Hell where the worst punishment is found.'*

I said: 'And if he kills another?' He (A) said: *'The punishment will be doubled for him.'*

Related from Abu Usamah Zayd al-Shahham, from Imam Saadiq (A), that the Messenger of Allah (S) stopped at Mina when he performed the

---

[34] *The Holy Qur'an*: The Table Spread (5): 32.
[35] *The Holy Qur'an*: The Table Spread (5): 32.

prayers there during the farewell pilgrimage when he said to his companions: *'What day is the most sacred?'*

They said: 'This day.'

He (S) said: *'And what month is most sacred?'*

They said: 'This month.'

He (S) said: *'And what land is the most sacred?'*

They said: 'This land.'

Then he (S) said:

> *'Then your blood and your wealth are sacred just as is this day and this month and this land are sacred until the day you will meet Him and he will ask you about your actions. Have I delivered the message?'*

They said: 'Yes'

He (S) said:

> *'Allah is a better witness to that. Whoever has been entrusted with something then he must return it to its owner; that the blood of a Muslim shall not be spilt nor his wealth taken except that which he gives out of the goodness of himself. Do not do injustice to yourselves and do not return to disbelief after I have gone.'*

Related from Abu Hamza al-Thumali, from Imam 'Ali ibn al-Hussein (A) who said:

> *'The Messenger of Allah (S) said: 'Do not take pride in a masterful warrior, for with Allah there is a killer (waiting for him) who has not died yet."*

Related from Jabir ibn Yazid, from Muhammad al-Baqir (A) who said:

> *'The Messenger of Allah (S) said: 'The first thing that Allah will pass judgement upon on the Day of Resurrection will be blood. The killer and the one he killed will be brought before him, then the blood relatives, then the people, until the one killed will come with his killer and will say: 'He killed me.' He will be asked: Did you kill him?, and he will not be able to conceal from Allah anything.'*

Related from Abu Jaroud, from Muhammad al-Baqir (A) who said:

> *'No soul will be killed except that it will be gathered on the Day of Resurrection attached to its killer by its right hand and to its head by the left hand with his veins pouring out blood. He will say to Allah: 'O Lord, ask him why he killed me.' If he killed him in obedience to Allah then the killer will be rewarded with Paradise and the one killed will be sent to the fire. If the killing was in obedience to another, the one killed will be told: 'Kill him as he killed you.' After that, Allah will do with him as He wishes.'*

Related from Hisham ibn Salim, from Ja'far al-Saadiq (A) who said:

> *'The believer remains within his religion as long as he does not spill sacred blood.'*

He also said: *'The one who kills a believer deliberately will not have his repentance accepted.'*

Author's note: That is he deserves not to have it accepted.

Related from 'Abdullah ibn Sanan, from Imam Saadiq (A) who said:

> *'Neither the shedder of blood, the drinker of wine, nor the backbiter will enter Paradise.'*

Related from Hanan ibn Sudeir, from Imam Saadiq (A) regarding Allah's words:

> **{ . . . Whosoever kills a person except for the murder of another or because of spreading corruption in the land, it is as if he has killed the people in their entirety.}**[36]

He (A) said: *'It is a valley in Hell which he will be in if he killed all the people and even if he killed one person he will be in it.'*

Related from Muhammad ibn Sanan from the answer Imam al-Ridha (A) gave to some of his questions: *'Allah has forbidden killing, for the reason that if the killing of people was allowed then the whole of creation would become corrupted and the people would be destroyed . . .'*

Related from Iban, from a source, who asked Imam Saadiq (A) about one who kills a person deliberately. He said: *'His reward is Hell.'*

Related from Hafs ibn al-Bakhtari, from Imam Saadiq (A):

'A woman was punished for a cat she had tied up until it died of thirst.'

---

[36] *The Holy Qur'an*: The Table Spread (5): 32.

Related from al-Halabi, from Imam Saadiq (A) who said:

> *'The most arrogant of people in the sight of Allah is one who kills someone other than is trying to kill him, or to beat someone who has not beaten him.'*

Relate from Suleiman ibn Khalid, who said: 'I heard Imam Saadiq (A) saying:

> *'Allah revealed through inspiration to Moses Son of 'Emran saying: 'O Moses, Say to the nation of the Children of Israel; Woe betide that you kill the sacred soul (the person) unjustly for whoever kills a person on Earth, I (meaning Allah) will kill him one-hundred thousand times in the same way he has killed his companion.'*

Author's note: This because the single seed can produce thousands of other seeds, for the Hereafter is the result of this worldly life.

Related from 'Abd al-Rahman ibn Muslim, from his father, who said: Imam Muhammad al-Baqir (A) said:

> *'Whoever kills a believer on purpose will have all his sins confirmed by Allah and the sins of the person he killed will be lifted from him, and this because of the quote in the Qur'an:*
>
> **{ . . . I intend that you are covered with my sin as well as yours and you will be of the Companions of the fire.}**[37]

Related from Ayyoub ibn 'Atiyyah al-Hudha who said: 'I heard Imam Saadiq (A) saying that

> *Imam 'Ali (A) found a letter in the scabbard of the Messenger of Allah's sword in which was written: 'The worst of people in the sight of Allah is the killer of one who does not fight him, and the one who beats one who does not beat him, and the one who pledges allegiance to other than his rightful allies, for he has committed the crime of Kufr (disbelief) in what Allah has sent down upon Muhammad (S). And whoever commits a crime or gives refuge to a criminal will not have his repentance nor his offer of compensation accepted and it is not allowed that a Muslim be given intercession in the case of a Hadd crime (a crime with a fixed punishment).*

---

[37] *The Holy Qur'an*: The Table Spread (5): 29.

Author's note: What is meant here by *kufr* is that of actions.

Al-Sayyid Murtada relates in his treatise *The Clear and the Ambiguous* (verses of the Qur'an), from the exegesis of al-Nu'mani with the chain of narration from Imam 'Ali (A) who said in a *hadith*: 'As regards those verses whose expression is particular but whose meaning is general, for the words of Allah:

> **{. . . and because of this We prescribed for the Sons of Isra'il that whoever kills a person except for the murder of another or for spreading corruption in the land, it is as if he has killed the people in their entirety.}**[38]

The expression (form) of the verse was revealed regarding the Children of Israel in particular but applies to all of creation in general to all the servants of Allah from the Children of Israel and all the other nations. This is a common occurrence in the Qur'an.

Related from Ja'far ibn Muhammad (A), from Zayd ibn Aslam, that the Messenger of Allah (S) was asked about the person who commits a crime or gives refuge to a criminal.' He said: *'He is the one who introduces an innovation into Islam, or kills except in Hadd (mandatory punishment), or plunders or steals something regarded as dear by the Muslims, or defends a criminal or aids and abets him.'*

Related from Ja'far ibn Muhammad (A), from his forefathers, in the will of the Prophet (S) to Imam 'Ali (A):

> *'He who joins up with those who are not his rightful allies will have the curse of Allah upon him. He who denies the labourer his rightful wage will have the curse of Allah upon him. He who commits a hadath (crime) or aids a criminal will have the curse of Allah upon him.' He was asked: 'O Messenger of Allah, what do you mean by this hadath?' He said: 'Murder . . . then he said: 'O 'Ali, the worst of people in the sight of Allah is the killer of one who does not fight him, or he who beats one who does not beat him, or he gives allegiance to other than his rightful allies. They have committed disbelief (kufr) in what Allah Almighty is He has sent down.'*

Related from Umayyah ibn Yazid, who said: 'The Messenger of Allah (S) said:

---

[38] *The Holy Qur'an*: The Table Spread (5): 32.

> *'Whoever commits a crime (hadath) or gives refuge to a criminal then the curse of Allah is upon him as well as that of the Angels and the people in general. Neither repentance nor compensation will be accepted from him.'* He was asked: 'What is this *hadath*?' He said: *'The killing of a person except for the murder of another, or mutilation in other than equal punishment (such as an eye for an eye), or the introduction of an innovation into the religion not part of the tradition (Sunnah), or the plundering or stealing of something regarded as dear.'*

Forbidding the taking part in killing

Related from Muhammad ibn Muslim, from Muhammad al-Baqir (A) who said:

> *'A man will come on the Day of Resurrection with a pot full to the brim of blood. He will say: By Allah I did not kill, nor did I take part in bloodshed. But he will be told: On the contrary, you mentioned (with foul intentions) my servant so-and-so. (That is in front of the one who killed him.)*

Related from Abu Hamza, from one of the Imams who said: 'The Messenger of Allah (S) arrived and he was told: 'O Messenger of Allah, there is a person murdered in *Juheinah*. The Messenger of Allah (S) stood up and walked until he reached their mosque (i.e. the people of *Juheinah*). The people heard about this and came to him. He said: *'Who has killed this person?'* They said: 'O Messenger of Allah, We do not know.' He said:

> *'One of the Muslims has been killed and no one knows who killed him! By He who has sent me with the truth, were the people of the Heavens and the Earth to take part in the killing of a Muslim and be content with that, Allah would throw them on their faces in the fire.'*

Related from Hamad ibn 'Uthman, from Imam Saadiq (A) who said:

> *'A man will come on the Day of Resurrection to another man and splatter his face with blood, when the people are being held to account for (their deeds).' He says: 'What have I and you got to do with it?' He (A) said: 'You aided (someone) against me on such and such a day with a word and I was killed.'*

Related from Ibn Abi 'Umeir, from others, from Imam Saadiq (A) who said:

> *'He who aids in the death of a believer even by a word will come on the Day of Resurrection and written between his eyes will be the words: 'Despaired of the Mercy of Allah.'*

Related from Mas'ada ibn Ziyad, from Ja'far ibn Muhammad (A), from his forefathers (A) that the Messenger of Allah (S) said:

> *'The worst of people on the Day of Resurrection is the muthallath.' He was asked: 'What O Messenger of Allah is the muthallath?' He (S) said: 'The man who strives against his brother and kills him for he will destroy himself and his brother and his guardian or leader.'*

Legalising the killing of a believer is equal to apostasy

Related from Sa'id al-Azraq, from Imam Saadiq (A) who said regarding a person who has killed a believer: *'He will be told: 'Die whatever death you wish to die. If you wish that of a Jew or if you wish that of a Nazarene.'*[39]

Related from Muhammad ibn Salim, from Muhammad al-Baqir (A) who said in a *hadith*:

> *'When Allah gave permission to His Messenger (S) to leave Mecca for Medina, He revealed the statutory punishments (hudud) and the mandatory acts and informed him of the acts of disobedience which Allah has made the Hellfire incumbent upon those who do them. He revealed the following verse regarding the killer:*
>
> **{. . . and as for he who kills a believer deliberately, his reward will be Hell abiding therein forever, and Allah's anger and curse will be upon him, and He has prepared for him a great torment.}**[40]

And Allah, Exalted is He, does not curse the believer:

---

[39] It is reported that in Hell there are separate quarters for the Muslims, Jews, Christians, etc. A Muslim murder would not even be allowed to carry the title of 'Muslim' there . . . he may chose another title.
[40] *The Holy Qur'an*: Women (4): 93.

> **{ . . . surely Allah curses the Infidels and has prepared for them an inferno, abiding therein always, they will neither find a friend nor a helper.}**[41]

Related from Imam 'Ali ibn al-Hussein (A), who said:

> *'The Messenger of Allah (S) said: 'Slandering the believer is a foul act, killing him is unbelief, eating his flesh*[42] *is disobeying Allah, and the sanctity of his wealth is as the sanctity of his blood.'*

Forbidding beating unjustly

Related from al-Halabi, from Imam Saadiq (A), who said:

> *'The worst of people in the sight of Allah is he who kills one who is not fighting him, or he who beats someone who has not beaten him.'*

Related from al-Muthanna, from Imam Saadiq (A) who said:

> *'In the scabbard of the Messenger of Allah's sword was found a document which said: 'The worst of men in the sight of Allah is the killer of one who does not fight him, or he who strikes someone who has not struck him, or one who claims lineage from someone other than his rightful father, for he does not believe in what has been revealed to Muhammad (S).'*

Related from al-Washa who said: 'I heard Imam al-Ridha (A) saying:

> *'The Messenger of Allah (S) said: 'Allah has cursed he who kills one who does not fight him, or strikes one who does not strike him.'*

Related from al-Thumali who said: The Imam (A) said:

> *'If a man beats another with a whip, Allah will beat him with a whip of fire.'*

Related from al-Fudeil ibn Sa'dan, from Imam Saadiq (A) who said:

> *'In the scabbard of the sword of the Messenger of Allah (S) was found a document which read: 'The curse of Allah and the Angels*

---

[41] *The Holy Qur'an*: The Coalitions (33): 64-65.

[42] Backbiting against someone is considered in the Qur'an and hadith as tantamount to eating that person's flesh.

> *and the People be upon the killer of one who does not fight him, or one who strikes one who does not strike him, or commits a crime, or gives refuge to a criminal.'*

Related from al-Hussein ibn Zayd, from al-Saadiq (A), from his forefathers, from the Prophet (S) in the *hadith* of the prohibitions that he said:

> *'He who strikes the cheek of a Muslim or his face, Allah will scatter his bones on the Day of Resurrection and he will be brought in chains to enter Hell, except if he has repented.'*

Related from al-Ridha (A), from his forefathers (A), from Imam 'Ali (A) who said:

> *'I inherited from the Messenger of Allah (S) two books; the book of Allah and a document in the scabbard of my sword.' He was asked: 'O Commander of the Faithful, what is this document in the scabbard of your sword?' He said: 'He who kills one not killing him, or strikes one not striking him will have the curse of Allah upon him.'*

Related from Imam 'Ali ibn Ja'far al-Ridha (A), from his brother Musa ibn Ja'far (A) who said:

> *'The people rushed to the scabbard of the sword of the Messenger of Allah after his death where they found a small document which read: 'He who gives refuge to a criminal is an unbeliever, and whoever pledges allegiance to other than his rightful allies will have the curse of Allah upon him. The worst of people in the sight of Allah is one who kills one not killing him or strikes one not striking him.'*

No to suicide

Related from Abu Wilad al-Hannat who said: 'I heard Imam Saadiq (A) saying:

> *'He who kills himself on purpose will be in the fire of Hell abiding therein forever.'*

Imam al-Saadiq (A) said:

> *'He who kills himself on purpose will be in the fire of Hell abiding therein forever, for Allah, Exalted is He has said:*

{. . . and do not kill yourselves, surely Allah is most merciful to you. Whomsoever does this out of enmity or oppression we will put him in a fire. This is an easy task for Allah.}[43]

Related from Abu Basir, from Muhammad al-Baqir (A) who said:

> *'One of the companions of the Messenger of Allah (S) called Qarnan, who used to help his brothers well, was mentioned in front of the Messenger of Allah who said, when his name was mentioned, that he was of the people of the fire. Someone came to the Messenger of Allah and said that Qarnan had been martyred. He (S) said: 'Allah will do with him as He wishes.' Then someone came and said that he had killed himself. The Messenger of Allah said: 'I bear witness that I am the Messenger of Allah.'*[44]

Related from Abu Sa'id al-Khudari who said: 'We used to go out on military excursions together in groups of twenty. We used to divide up the work; some of us handled the baggage, others doing tasks for our companions, watering the beasts and making food, and another group used to go to the Prophet (S). It so happened that there was a man amongst us who used to do the work of three men; sewing, watering the animals, and making the food. This was mentioned to the Prophet (S) who said: *'This man is destined for the fire.'* We subsequently met with the enemy and fought with them. This man went out and took an arrow and killed himself with it. The Prophet (S) said: *'I bear witness that I am the Messenger of Allah and His servant.'*

Related from Najiah, from Muhammad al-Baqir (A) who said in a *hadith*: *'The believer will be tried to the utmost and will die to the utmost but he does not kill himself.'*

The parent may not kill his child even if illegitimate

Related from Ibrahim ibn Abi al-Balad, from Imam Saadiq (A) who said:

> *'During the time of Amir-ul-Mu'mineen, there was a pious woman called Umm Qanan. One of the companions of 'Ali came to her and found her aggrieved so he said to her: 'Why is it I find*

---

[43] *The Holy Qur'an*: Women (4): 29-30.

[44] This is to indicate that the Messenger of Allah (S) had foretold of Qarnan's position before receiving the report of his suicide from the people. That is the Messenger of Allah (S) knows the unseen by the will of Allah.

you aggrieved?' She said: 'I recently buried a friend of mine but the earth spat her out twice.' So the man went to Amir-ul-Mu'mineen 'Ali (A) and related the story to him. He said: 'The earth will accept the Jew or the Christian so what is up with her other than her being tormented with Allah's torment?' Then he said: 'If she was to take the earth from the grave of a Muslim man and throw it on her grave she will be still.' So the man went to Umm Qanan and told her what to do so she took some earth from the grave of a Muslim man and threw it on her grave and she was still. The man asked about her and he was told that she had a strong love for men; no sooner would she give birth that she would throw her child in the oven."

The prohibition of abortion

Related from Ishaq ibn 'Ammar who said: 'I said to Imam 'Ali (A):

> *'What of the woman who fears pregnancy so she drinks some potion which ejects what is in her belly?'* He said: *'No.'* I said: 'But it is only a sperm drop.' He said: *'The first thing that is created is the sperm drop.'*

Killing a believer for his faith is a serious crime

Related from Imam Saadiq (A) who was asked about whether repentance can be accepted from a believer who has killed another believer deliberately. He said:

> *'If he killed him for his faith then there is no repentance for him. If he was killed out of anger or for another worldly reason then his repentance is that he pays blood money and he should go to the blood relatives and confess to the killing of their relative. If they choose to forgive him and do not kill him then he should pay the compensation, and set free a slave, and fast two consecutive months, and feed sixty indigents as a repentance to Allah Exalted is He.'*

Author's note: What is meant by 'there is no repentance for him' is that the seriousness of the crime is such that it is as if there is no way of repentance for him, whereas as the evidences have shown, repentance may be accepted for all sins.

Related from Sama'a, from Imam Saadiq (A) who was asked about Allah Almighty's words:

> **{. . . and as for he who kills a believer deliberately, his reward will be Hell.}**[45]

He said: *'Whoever kills a believer because of his religion is that deliberate killer about whom Allah says:*

> **{ . . . and He (Allah) has prepared for him a mighty torment.}**[46]

I (Sama'a) said: 'What of the man who has a disagreement with another man such that he strikes him with his sword and kills him?' He (A) said: *'This is not the deliberate killer referred to by Allah Exalted and Majestic is He.'*

The expiation for the killing of the believer

Related from 'Isa al-Darir, who said: 'I said to Imam Saadiq (A): 'How can the man who has killed another on purpose repent?' He said: *'He should give himself up (to the blood relatives).'* I said: 'He fears that they will kill him.' He said: *'Then let him pay them compensation.'* I said: *'He fears they will kill him.'* He said: *'Then let him put the compensation money in a purse and wait for the time of prayer then throw the purse into their house.'*

Ismail al-Ja'fi relates that he asked Muhammad al-Baqir (A) about the man who kills another on purpose. He (A) said: *'There are three acts of expiation upon him; to free a slave, to fast two consecutive months, and to feed sixty indigents.'* Imam 'Ali ibn al-Hussein (A) gave the same ruling.

Related from Abu al-Ma'za, from Imam Saadiq (A) about the man who kills a servant accidentally. He said: *'He should set free a slave, fast two consecutive months, and give alms to sixty indigents.'* He also said: *'If he is not able to free a slave then let him fast, and if he is not able to fast then let him pay the alms.'*

Related by Sama'a who asked the Imam (A) about whether there is a way to repentance for one who kills another on purpose. He said: *'No, not until he pays the blood money to the relatives, frees a slave, fasts two*

---

[45] *The Holy Qur'an*: Women (4): 93.
[46] *The Holy Qur'an*: Women (4): 93.

consecutive months, asks Allah's forgiveness and offers voluntary prayers. If he does this then I would hope that his repentance would be accepted.' I (Sama'a) said: 'And if he has no money?' He (A) said: *He should ask the Muslims for money so that he can pay the compensation to the blood relatives.'*

Related by al-Halabi, from Imam Saadiq (A) in a *hadith* that he asked about a man who had killed his slave. He said: *'He should set free a slave, fast two consecutive months, then he shall have repentance.'*

The consequences of killing a believer

Related from Ja'far ibn Muhammad (A), from his father, from Imam 'Ali (A) who said:

> *'The Messenger of Allah (S) said: 'There is a valley in Hell named Sa'ir which if opened the fires will roar from it. Allah has prepared it for the murderers.'*

Related from al-Saadiq (A) who said:

> *'Allah inspired to Moses Son of 'Emran to say to the nation of the children of Israel: 'Woe betide that you kill the sacred person unjustly. Whoever kills a person in this world will be killed in the fire one-hundred thousand times in the same way that he killed his companion.'*

Related from Amir-ul-Mu'mineen (A) that he said about Allah's words narrating about the People of the fire:

> **{ . . . Lord, show us those of the jinn and men who led us astray so that we may put them under our feet and they be the lowest.}**[47]

He (A) said:

> *'This refers to Iblis (the chief Satan) and that son of Adam who killed his brother, for these are the first to sin from the jinn and from men.'*

He (A) who said:

> *'The shedding of blood unjustly brings about the vengeance of Allah and an end to His blessings.'*

---

[47] *The Holy Qur'an:* Explained (41): 29.

Related from the Holy Prophet (S) who said:

> *'Never does the Earth cry to its Lord so much as when sacred blood is spilt upon it.'*

He (S) said:

> *'The killing of a believer is greater in the sight of Allah than the perishing of the world.'*

He (S) said:

> *'The victim of murder will come (on the Day of Resurrection) with his killer pouring blood onto his face and Allah will say: 'You killed him.' And the killer will not be able to conceal any speech from Allah so he will be ordered into the fire.'*

He (S) said:

> *'The first thing that Allah will look at on the Day of Resurrection will be blood.'*

Related from Ibn 'Abbas who said: 'I heard the Prophet (S) saying:

> *'The victim of killing will come on the Day of Resurrection with one of his hands attached to his head and the other attached to his killer and his veins will be pouring with blood. They will be brought before the throne and the victim will say to Allah Blessed and Exalted is He: 'O Lord, he killed me.' Allah Almighty is He will say to the killer: 'You miserable wretch.' And he will be ordered into the fire.'*

The Prophet (S) said in a *hadith*:

> *'At the time when a killer kills (a believer), he cannot be a believer.'"*[48]

In another *hadith* he (S) said:

> *'The most detestable of people in the sight of Allah are an apostate in the sacred precinct, one who follows the way of the days of ignorance after Islam, and one who spills blood unjustly.'*

He (S) said:

---

[48] This is to indicate that a true Muslim does not commit murder and if he does he is not a Muslim.

> *'The perishing of the world is lesser in the sight of Allah than the killing of a believer.'*

He (S) said:

> *'The first thing that will be passed judgement upon on the Day of Resurrection will be blood.'*

Related from Ayyub ibn Nuh, from Imam al-Ridha (A), from his forefathers who said:

> *'The Messenger of Allah (S) said: 'There are five types of people whose fires will never be extinguished nor their bodies die (in the fire): A man who commits shirk, a man who displeases his parents, a man who takes his brother to the ruler who kills him, a man who kills his brother unjustly, and a man who sins and blames his sin on Allah Almighty.'*

Related by Zayd ibn Arqam as saying: 'We were with the Messenger of Allah (S) on the day of Ghadir Khum when we were holding the branches of trees above his head and he (S) said:

> *'May Allah curse one who claims lineage form one other than his rightful father, or who pledges allegiance to other than his rightful allies, after having heard me and seen me. Let he who lies about what I have said deliberately prepare himself a seat in the fire. Your blood and wealth are sacrosanct just as this day and this land and this month are sacred.'*

Also related from the Prophet (S) that he gave a sermon when he wanted to go out to Tabuk saying after praising Allah:

> *'O people, The most truthful of speech is the book of Allah . . . (until he said) slandering a believer is a foul act, fighting a believer is tantamount to unbelief, eating the flesh of a believer*[49] *is a grave sin, the sanctity of his wealth is as the sanctity of his blood.'*

It is reported that when the Messenger of Allah (S) was brought a victim killed, who had been found in the vicinity of the Ansar, he said: *'Is he known?'* They said: 'Yes, O Messenger of Allah.' He said: *'If the whole nation were to take part in the killing of a believer, Allah would throw them into the fire of Hell.'*

---

[49] In Qur'an and hadith backbiting against someone is referred to as eating one's flesh.

Also related from the Prophet (S) who said:

> *'Whoever aids the killing of a Muslim even through a single word, will arrive on the Day of Resurrection despairing of the Mercy of Allah.'*

Related from Abu Sa'id al-Khudari, who said: 'During the time of the Messenger of Allah (S) a man was found dead. He (S) came out angrily and mounted the pulpit. He praised Allah and then he said:

> *'A Muslim has been killed and it is not known who killed him? By Him who holds my soul in His hands, were the people of the heavens and the earth to take part in the killing of a believer or to approve of such a killing, Allah would put them in the fire. By Him who holds my soul in His hands, no-one shall whip another but that he will be whipped tomorrow (in the hereafter) in the fire of Hell.'*

Related from the Prophet (S) who said:

> *'If the people of the seven heavens and the seven earths were to take part in the spilling of a believer's blood, Allah would throw them all into the fire.'*

Related from Muhammad ibn Muslim who said: 'I heard Muhammad al-Baqir (A) saying:

> *'The servant of Allah will be brought on the Day of Resurrection and the blood he has spilled will be given to him and he will be told: 'This is your share of the blood of so-and-so.' He will say: 'O Lord, You took my life I had never spilled any blood.' He will be told: 'On the contrary, you heard from so-and-so such and such a thing which you repeated and it was repeated by others until a certain tyrant heard about it who killed him for it so this is your share of his blood.'*

In one account it is said that when the Khawarij left al-Hurur they assembled the people and killed the righteous servant of Allah 'Abdullah ibn Janab ibn al-Arth, Imam 'Ali's governor of Nahrawan. They slaughtered him on the bank of the river above a pig and said: *'the killing of you and this pig is the same to us.'* They also cut open the belly of his pregnant wife and slaughtered her and they killed her suckling child before him. Imam 'Ali (A) was informed of this, so he returned to Nahrawan and appealed to their better nature but they refused all but to fight him. He asked them about the killing of Ibn Janab and they confessed to it one after another and said we will kill you as we have killed him. Imam 'Ali (A) said: *'By Allah, if all the people of the world confessed to killing him and I was able to kill them I would do so.'*

Author's note: What is meant is their taking part in the sin of killing.

Related from Ishaq ibn 'Ammar, from Imam Saadiq (A) that he read the following Qur'anic verse:

> **{. . . this because they used to disbelieve in the signs of Allah, and kill the Prophets unjustly, this because they disobeyed and were transgressors.}**[50]
>
> He said: *'By Allah, they did not strike them with their hands nor did they kill them with their swords but they listened to their speeches and broadcast them (to their enemies). They were then arrested and killed because of those reporting and therefore the reporting and broadcasting were tantamount to killing, transgressing, and disobedience.'*

Related from Amir-ul-Mu'mineen (A) who said:

> *'One who approves of the action of a people is as one who has taken part in the act with them. There are two sins for he who enters into a wrong act – the sin of approving of it and the sin of actually doing it.'*

He (A) said: *'He who aids and abets in the killing of a believer has taken himself out of Islam.'*

He (A) said: *'The most despicable of people in the sight of Allah is he who beats a Muslim unjustly.'*

Related from Mas'ada ibn Sadaqah, from Imam Saadiq (A) who said:

> *'Amir-ul-Mu'mineen 'Ali (A) said: "O people, Allah, Blessed and Exalted is He, has sent to you the Messenger (the Prophet Muhammad (S)), and revealed to him the Book in truth while you were in oblivious about the Book and He who sent it, and about the Messenger and He who sent him after a period of absence of messengers, and suffering of the nations, and spread of ignorance . . . . ."* until he said " . . . *and the world has turned against its people in anger, turning away from them and not towards them. Its fruit is commotion, and its food carrion. Its slogan is fear, and*

---

[50] *The Holy Qur'an*: The Heifer (2): 61.

its garment is sword. You were torn to pieces. It blinded the eyes of its people, and prolonged its days (of misery) over them. They severed their bonds of kinship, shed each other's blood, and buried alive their own female infants. They choose their own pleasure and comfort over their children's (existence). They do not seek any reward from Allah, nor do they fear Allah's punishment. When they are alive they are blind and ill-mannered, and when they are dead, they are hopeless in Hell."

Related from Ali ibn Ibrahim regarding Allah's words:

{ . . . and when the girl child buried alive will be asked for what sin was she killed.}[51]

He said: 'The Arabs used to kill their girl children out of jealousy so on the Day of Resurrection the girl buried alive will ask for what sin was she killed?'

Related from the Messenger of Allah (S) that he said:

'The gravest of major sins is to assign partners to Allah when He has himself created them. Then it is to kill your child for fear that it will eat with you.'

Related from 'Abdullah ibn Mas'oud who said the Prophet (S) said:

'The worst of people in the sight of Allah is the killer of one who does not fight him, or one who kills within the sacred precinct, or the killer in revenge for something in the days of ignorance (pre-Islamic era).'

Related in the exegesis of Ali ibn Ibrahim regarding Allah Almighty's words:

{. . . and as for he who kills a believer deliberately, his reward will be Hell abiding therein forever, and Allah's anger and curse will be upon him, and He has prepared for him a great torment.}[52]

He (A) said: *'Whoever kills a believer for his faith will not have his repentance accepted. Whoever kills a prophet or the Wasi*[53] *of a prophet will not have his repentance accepted for there is no one similar to him for the retaliatory killing. It may be that a man*

---

[51] *The Holy Qur'an*: Extinguished (81): 8-9.
[52] *The Holy Qur'an*: Women (4): 93.
[53] A Wasi is the successor appointed by the prophet.

> *of the Polytheists, Jews or Christians kills a man for being a Muslim, but if he enters Islam, Allah will erase the sin from him because of the Messenger of Allah saying: 'Islam annuls what has gone before it.'*

That is, it erases what has gone before because the greatest of sins in the sight of Allah is *shirk* and if repentance for this sin is accepted upon entering Islam then it follows that repentance for all other sins is also accepted.

As for al-Saadiq's words: *'He will not have a way to repentance.'* This means that whoever kills a prophet or *wasi* will not have a way to repentance because there is no one like the prophet or *wasi* to have the blood retaliation carried out upon him so one who kills a prophet or *wasi* will not be granted repentance.

Muhammad ibn Ali ibn Shahr Ashub relates in the book *al-Manaqib* saying: 'Al-Zuhri was an agent of the Umayyad Clan. He punished a man who died of the punishment. Al-Zuhri fled to the desert. He entered a cave where he spent nine years. Then 'Ali ibn al-Hussein (A) made the Hajj pilgrimage and al-Zuhri approached him. 'Ali ibn al-Hussein (A) said to him: *'I fear for you that you despair (the mercy of Allah) more than I fear for your sin. Send a compensation to the family of the man you killed and return to your family and attend to the affairs of your religion and adhere to them.'* He (al-Zuhri) said to him: 'You have relieved me O Master. **Allah knows best where and how to carry His message.**[54] He returned to his house and became a follower of Imam 'Ali ibn al-Hussein (A) and was known as one of his companions.

[54] *The Holy Qur'an:* The Cattle (6): 124.

Part Two

In this paper the author addresses the Islamic movement in particular because of the difference of opinions there is amongst the various groups and sects of the movement. Otherwise he calls upon all Muslims, and upon all mankind for that matter, to adhere to peaceful and non-violent means in all aspects of life.

In line with his political views, Imam Shirazi calls for the creation of an international Islamic reform movement in order to help attain the salvation of the Muslim Community, as this can be seen in many of his works. Subsequently this in turn would then facilitate the salvation of mankind in general. In this work he emphasises on the Islamic movement although his discussions on peace and non-violence usually take up a more general tune. Imam Shirazi then goes on to emphasise that such a movement must adopt peaceful policies in all aspects and domains . . .

This paper is an extract from Chapter 4 of Imam Shirazi's book ***Towards Islamic Revival*** pages 141 – 174. Chapter 4 of this book discusses Axiom 4 of the 6 axioms the author envisages for the Islamic movement.

Translated by Ali Adam

Islamic Movement and Peace

The Movement Must be Peaceful

The motto of Islam is 'peace'. Hence when one Muslim meets with another he will say to him: *'al-Salam Alaykum'* meaning 'Peace be upon you' and the other will answer: *'Alaykum al-Salam'* 'Upon you be Peace.' And in the same way that he begins with a greeting of peace upon his brother, he will end his meeting with a farewell greeting of peace, saying when he wishes to leave: 'Peace be upon you.' Islam then is the religion of peace, hence Allah, Exalted is He, says in the Holy Qur'an: **{Enter into a state of peace one and all.}** (2:208)

Wars, blockades, and other forms of violence are only emergency measures and not the norm and they go against basic Islamic principles. Their nature is that of dire necessity as in the eating of 'unlawful meat' or the like and the basic principle is that of peace. Hence in Islam, war is taken at face value. However, despite this, Allah Almighty says: **{And whoever assaults you then assault him in the same way that he assaults you.}** (2:194) Then in another place He says: **{But to forgive is closer to piety.}** (2:273)

The way of the Prophet (S) and Fatima (A) and the impeccable Imams (A) was thus. Peace was their watchword in all their affairs and even in their battles, and the unparalleled success of the Prophet of Islam (S) and the Imams (A) was for reasons all stemming from the peace that they endowed themselves with in all their affairs.

Hence we find that the 'Abbasids, Umayyads, and Ottomans proceeded in a way that only earned them an ill reputation. Whereas the true leaders of Islam have only a good reputation and are known by the people for peace, kindness and forgiveness:

We ruled and forgiveness *was our nature, when you ruled blood flowed as a river flows.*

Enough for you now is this difference between us, for every vessel will show what substance it holds.

The fact that Islam encompasses peace is one of the reasons for its initial progress and for its second age of progress after the attacks of the Crusaders from the west and the Moguls from the east. And through peace we hope for the advancement of Islam in this century which has been so full of attacks from east and west alike on its lands.

The Messenger of Allah, Muhammad (S), progressed, as we have said, through peace that he adopted as a mantra. One example of this is Mecca[55], the capital of unbelief and idolatry and the capital of waging war against the Messenger of Allah (S). The people of Mecca confronted the Messenger of Allah by every possible means. They banished him, killed his daughter Zaynab, confiscated his wealth and killed many of his followers. Finally they tried to assassinate him so he fled secretly to Madinah but they continued their plots against his holy mission. Despite this, after more than twenty years, when the Messenger (S) wanted to conquer Mecca, he made preparations then proceeded to conquer that city peacefully without one drop of blood being spilt. Among the preparations he made were when he took possession of Khaibar, he took as spoils a large hoard of golden vessels as many as twenty thousand in number and of differing sizes. The Messenger (S) sent a number of these vessels to be shared out amongst the poor of Mecca even though they were unbelievers, polytheists, and warring against the Messenger of Allah (S). When these golden vessels arrived for the people of Mecca, they were confused and amazed. They said: 'We fight this man, we confiscate his property, we kill his followers and his relatives and he deals with us in such a kind manner.'

This was an overture from the Messenger of Allah (S) to bring Islam to Mecca and to destroy the idols and to establish peace between the people. When the Messenger of Allah (S) conquered Mecca, Abu Sufyan, his archenemy, came and the Messenger of Allah (S) pardoned him. Not only this but he made his house a sanctuary saying: 'Whoever enters the house of Abu Sufyan is safe.' Then he turned to the wife of Abu Sufyan, Hind, the woman famous for her immoral acts and attacks on the Messenger of Allah (S). She who had torn open the abdomen of Master of the Martyrs Hamza, and amputated his ears and his nose and mutilated him in the most vile manner, taking out his liver and chewing it in her mouth. This woman, this 'war criminal' was sent by the Messenger of Allah a document of pardon. By this, the Messenger of Allah (S) recorded the most magnificent example in the history of creation of forgiveness even of his most ardent enemies. The Messenger of Allah (S) accepted the Islam of Hind and he made it a condition upon

---

[55] The peace treaty between the Muslim and Quraysh (the Muslims' adversaries) was broken by Quraysh, and this consequently lead to the peaceful conquest of Mecca without any bloodletting.

her that she should not prostitute herself which points to the fact that she was a famous prostitute before Islam. The noble Qur'anic verse, which the Messenger of Allah (S) recited to Hind, also points to this fact where Allah says:

{And if the believing women come to you to pledge their allegiance to you on the basis that they do not associate partners with Allah, nor steal, nor commit adultery . . .} (60:12)

Similarly, the Messenger of Allah (S) forgave the people of Mecca and spoke the historical words: 'Go ye for you are at liberty.' He did not seek to reclaim his houses or the houses of his companions that had been confiscated by the Polytheists. And when he took the key to the Ka'bah from the custodian, the Qur'anic verse was revealed: **{Allah orders you to convey all things held in trust to their rightful owners.}** (4:58), as some exegeses have said, and after he destroyed the idols he returned the key to the custodian.

The Messenger of Allah (S) also opened the way to bring Khalid (Ibn al-Walid) to the religion by saying to his brother Walid ibn al-Walid: 'I am amazed at your brother Khalid, he is a clever man, why has he not entered Islam?, And why has he not said the two testaments of faith (*shahadatayn*)?' When Walid came to his brother Khalid, and conveyed to him the speech of the Messenger of Allah (S) about him, Khalid was amazed that the Messenger of Allah (S) would seek to win him over with such kindness since he had been fighting a full-scale war against the Messenger of Allah (S). This became a reason for Khalid accepting Islam and joining the Muslim army as is well documented in the chronicles.

Through this peaceful means, the Messenger of Allah (S) gained dominion over the hearts of the people of Mecca before he gained dominion over their bodies. And when he did gain dominion over their bodies, they followed his lead and obeyed him and said of him: He is a noble brother and the son of a noble brother.

The chroniclers report that Mecca at this time was the capital of unbelief and Polytheism, hypocrisy and blood letting, selfishness and pride. When it surrendered to the Messenger of Allah (S), most of the people did not announce their entry into Islam but rather remained on the way of Polytheism. The Messenger of Allah (S) did not coerce them to accept Islam ever but instead left them to themselves so that they would live by themselves under the rule of Islam to enter Islam in the future.

The Messenger of Allah (S) made a man named 'Atab the governor of Mecca. He was a young Muslim man of deep faith who was nearly twenty years of age. He fixed the sum of nearly two talent of Silver as a daily pay for him.

The chroniclers mention that Mecca no longer made war after that and succumbed to the rule of 'Atab without any need for an army or security force or force of arms or other power. This because the Messenger of Allah (S) had gained hold of their minds and hearts and the heart, if it becomes allied to a person is not able to rebel or resist. In this way, the people of Mecca began to sense the correctness of the Islamic way and that in it they would still have their authority and leadership and their honour and their wealth would remain in their own hands and their sacred objects would remain sacred.

Sa'ad ibn 'Ubada took the banner during the first moments of the conquest of Mecca. Then he began traversing the streets of Mecca proclaiming: 'Today is the day of slaughter, today the women will be captured.' When the Messenger of Allah (S) heard this he said to Imam 'Ali ibn Abi Talib (A): 'O 'Ali, take the banner from Sa'ad and proclaim the opposite.' Imam 'Ali (A) then took the banner from the hand of Sa'ad and began to proclaim in the streets and alleys of Mecca: 'Today is the day of mercy, today the honour of the women will be protected.' Meaning that today we have come to you with mercy and to unite your ranks and to bring about a brotherhood between you, and today your women will remain with their honour and their chastity. These actions of the Messenger of Allah (S) were a prime cause for the unparalleled submission of the holy city of Mecca to the Messenger of Allah (S).

War, accusation, slander, backbiting, insinuation, enmity, hatred, egotism, pride, deception and the like are the causes of the decline of nations and individuals alike. On the contrary, the human being is a slave to virtues. Imam Amir-ul-Mu'mineen (A) says: '*I wonder at he who buys slaves with his wealth, why does he not buy the freemen with his morals?*'

In any case, it is imperative that the Islamic movement that is striving to establish a worldwide Islamic state adopts peace as its mantra and syllabus and method to attract the widest possible audience. Through this God's aid and assistance may be achieved.

The Noble Consequences of Peace

Those involved in the Islamic movement must be characterised by peace in their thought processes, in their speech, and in their actions in dealing with both the enemy and the friend. For the consequences of peace are noblest and it is fastest in reaching the desired goal. Peace and peace making are principles which bring about the advancement of the peacemaker. Whereas the non-peace-maker or the violent person will always remain behind.

The greatest Prophet (S) said to Imam 'Ali: '*O 'Ali, the noble traits of this world and the next are mildness of speech, magnanimity, and the forgiveness of he who wrongs you.*'

What is not meant here is the forgiveness of the unjust transgressor who does not repent, but rather it is the forgiveness when in power. The poet has turned these words of the Messenger of Islam into verse form saying:

The noblest of virtues are epitomised in three;
Mild speech, magnanimity, and such forgiveness as can be.

Meaning that if one is in position of power, to forgive and pardon he should do so, and be mild in speech not violent which, if he was, he would end up being distanced from the people.

In another *hadith* in praise of the faithful it is said that the believers are: 'humble', meaning that they are humble and not so unpleasant that the people will fear to be around them and beside them, for the violent unpleasant person is generally avoided by the people.

The (Islamic) movement which wishes to bring together the people and guide them to the straight path ought to adopt mildness, for the people will gather round he who is humble, mild, cheerful and friendly as is found in the *hadith* about the qualities of the believer: '*The believer is humble, mild, cheerful and friendly, joy is on his face, sadness in his heart.*' This is how the person who seeks to gather the people should be. If the motto of the movement was to be violence, the movement would lose all legality in the eyes of the people and they will come to think that just as the movement is violent against its enemies, it will inevitably become violent against them some day. The poet says:

Have patience in the face of the envious, for your patience will kill him,
Just as the fire will eat itself up if it does not find that which will fuel him.

This is a fact. The violent person acts violently with friend, foe and stranger alike, whereas the mild person acts mildly with both friend and enemy. Hence many *hadiths* carry the commendation of mildness, gentleness, compassion, and love. It is related from the Prophet Jesus (A) in a beautiful speech attributed to him: '*You have been told to love thy friends, but this is not what is important, for even the tithe collectors love their friends. I say to you love thine enemies.*' It is clear from the speech of Jesus that this does not result in benefiting the enemy as much as it results in benefiting the person himself, for the person who loves his enemy will try to establish good relations and a connection with him which is what can cause the enemy to cease his enmity.

There is a *hadith* from the Messenger of Allah (S) which says: '*Give gifts to each other, establish love between one another*', meaning that the giving of gifts to each other causes mutual love to be established between people. There are many other *hadiths* in the same vein reported from the Prophets and the Imams (Upon whom be peace).

The Islamic movement must then be characterised by peace and make peace its motto so that people may have confidence in it. Any movement which carries out a violent act or two violent acts will be blamed by the people for any subsequent violent acts which appear in society, just as the thief who has stolen once will be blamed for other thefts that take place. In the proverb: '*The mind connects a thing with the most general and the usual.*' If the movement is the subject of the suspicion of the people who connect it with violence and the like then the people will desert it and it will not be able to reach its goal.

As well as adopting the conditions of creating awareness, organisation, and observing general principles, the Islamic movement must also be based upon the following four foundations of peace and peace-making, mildness, compassion, and kindness. The *hadith* and traditions of the Messenger of Allah (S), his story, his history, his battles and military campaigns all make clear how mild and peaceful he was and the fine results he gained because of this.

For example, we can see how the Messenger of Allah (S) after conquering Mecca dealt with the city's people in such a kind and lofty way that he was able to achieve two things:

The first is that he was able to loan from Safwan ibn Umayyah, one of the major Polytheists, four hundred suits of armour. During the Age of Ignorance, Safwan had been in the position of the minister of war for the Polytheists and he had many suits of armour which he would supply to the fighters in the wars which took place between the tribes and clans. When the Messenger of Allah (S) requested from Safwan that he lend him this armour he had no hesitation in giving them to the Prophet because he had experienced his kindness and tasted peace under him during the conquest of Mecca.

The second, the Prophet (S) was able to create an army of two thousand men who were with him on the battle of Hunein which happened directly after the conquest of Mecca. Thirty thousand warriors from the tribe of Huwazin and other tribes had gathered in the valley of Hunein near Mecca to attack the Messenger and kill him and his companions. The Prophet had with him ten thousand of the Mujahidin from Madinah and the two thousand men from Mecca making in all twelve thousand fighters, warriors, horsemen, and armoured men. Hence the Messenger was able to fight the people of Hunein in this bitter war, which the Holy Qur'an mentions.

The Messenger of Allah (S), with his companions from Madinah, and those who had joined up with him from Mecca, was able to rout the enemy army and provide a victory for Islam, and this ended the resistance of the unbelievers throughout the entire Arabian Peninsula. This is because of the morals of the Prophet and his peacefulness, his compassion, kindness, open-handedness, truthfulness, and trustworthiness.

After the battle of Hunein had ended, he returned the armour to Safwan. The Muslims had won in this battle a great deal of booty and the chronicles report that Safwan looked at the camels, which had been won by the Messenger of Allah (S). The Messenger saw this and said: 'Do you desire these camels O Safwan.' He said: 'Yes O Messenger of Allah.' So the Messenger said: 'Give Safwan ten of the camels', so they gave him ten. Then he said: 'And another ten', and he continued to give him until he had given one hundred camels to Safwan.

In truth, this giving was to the people of Mecca as a whole because Safwan had an important family and relatives and in those days when the chieftain obtained something it meant that his followers and family would also obtain a share in that thing.

In this way, the Messenger of Allah (S) was able to draw the attention of the Polytheists in Mecca and they began to enter into Islam and testify the two testaments of faith without violence or warfare and without the spilling of blood but rather out of love for Islam, for they saw in Islam a refuge and a shelter, and leadership, friendship, wealth, fraternity, and a lessening of problems. Hence, the Islamic movement must learn from the Messenger of Allah (S) how to act and make peace.

Peace . . . always

To continue the discussion about the peaceful treatment of the friend and the foe, which is one of the vital fundamentals upon which the struggles of the international Islamic movement should be based, peace initially is bitter and difficult. It requires self-control, forgiveness, and turning a blind eye, and the capacity to act decisively and in the best possible way.

Allah Almighty has said, in the Holy Qur'an:

{Repel (evil) with that which is best for then you will find that your former enemy will become your warmest ally. But none shall achieve this but the patient ones and none shall achieve this except one blessed with great fortune.} (41:34-35)

One should always be looking towards the goal and realise that revenge inhibits the reaching of that goal. Hence we see that the Prophets and Imams (A) and reformers always tended towards peace not only before they had power but even after they had power.

The well known tradition reports that the Messenger of Allah (S) was extremely angry at Wahshi the killer of Hamza (A) who was one of the stalwarts of Islam as indeed were ‘Ali and Ja’far, the sons of Abu Talib. They were the staunch supporters of the Messenger of Allah (S) and his assistants in his wars and military campaigns and they had a position of pride and honour amongst the Muslims. Because of this, Hind, the wife of Abu Sufyan said to al-Wahshi: ‘If you kill Muhammad, or ‘Ali, or Hamza I will reward you with such and such and I will free you from your bondage.’ Al-Wahshi replied: ‘As for Muhammad, I cannot kill him because his companions surround him. As for ‘Ali, I have no way against him for when he enters the field (of battle) he is so self aware that nothing escapes his notice be it in front, to his right or left or behind him. But I am able to kill Hamza for when he enters the field he is not self-aware. He entered the battle and took advantage of him and attacked him. Hence Hamza was killed in that vile way, and Hind made a horrible example of him. Because of this, the Messenger of Allah (S) became very angry at Wahshi. Then one of his companions came to him after a time and said: ‘O Messenger of Allah (S) will you forgive Wahshi, for he desires Islam.’ The Messenger of Allah said: ‘Then I forgive him.’ Indeed the Messenger of Allah (S) did forgive him and he entered Islam and became a good Muslim. He (Wahshi) used to say after that: 'I must aid Islam as I used to aid unbelief against Islam.' Wahshi took part in battles and had an important role. He took part in the story of al-Yamamah and he served Islam as he used to serve unbelief against Islam.

Hence we can see the excellent consequences, which arose from the forgiveness of the Messenger of Allah and his acceptance of the Islam of Wahshi.

In the same vein, the Messenger of Allah (S) also forgave Habbar who was one of the most uncouth of the people of Mecca and one who had stirred up trials and tribulations for the Muslims. He had caused the death of Zaynab, the daughter of the Messenger of Allah (S) who was a pious woman who resembled the Messenger of Allah (S) in her morals and her looks as she resembled her mother Khadijah (A). She was with a child when Habbar caused her fall from the saddle and the child miscarried. She remained ill because of this until her death. The Messenger of Allah (S) was aggrieved at this and called for Habbar's blood and when he conquered Mecca, Habbar fled to the mountains because the Prophet had said: 'Kill Habbar even if he is clinging to the curtains of the Ka'bah.' This because he was considered to be an ill-mannered uncouth person who stirred up trials as we previously mentioned.

Then a man came to the Messenger of Allah (S) and said: 'O Messenger of Allah, you have forgiven everyone, so forgive Habbar also. You are most forgiving and noble.' The Prophet said: 'I forgive him.'

History records the kindness of the Messenger of Allah (S) and his patience and his decisiveness. These noble qualities deserve to be recorded as miracles. How great the man must be to reach this state where he forgives the killer of his uncle Hamza and the killer of his daughter and his still born grandson – Zaynab and her child.

Because of this we see that Islam began to spread because the ethics of Islam shone out impressing the people. This is the type of Islam that a person should believe in, the type, which around whose banner he is able to rally in all goodness and peace.

The international Islamic movement must colour itself with the same tint of forgiveness, peacefulness, peace, and peace-making. Not just with its friends and relatives, but also with strangers, and enemies as we see in the stories of the great reformers.

One Muslim commander took control of some territory after a civil war and a rebellion. A group of officers who were considered to be war criminals were arrested and sentenced to death by execution. When that chief, that patient, honest, kind, and intelligent man, took the death warrant he threw it to the floor and said: 'To have those officers above ground alive is better than to have them below ground dead. I grant them free pardon so set them free.' Those who had brought the death warrant were amazed but they could not disobey his orders so they went and freed the officers. Then these officers became the most earnest servants of Islam. They served their homeland in another war after that as an expiation for their previous ill acts. The chief said: 'Do you see how effective kindness, patience, forgiveness and peace can be. If we had ordered the death of those officers, who would have led the army? Who would have defeated our enemy when they attacked us?'

So it is imperative that the watchword of the Islamic movement be 'peace' in word, deed, and writing, and peace in all circumstances and with all the people.

Peace: The Way of the Prophets and the Imams

Since the principle of peace is such a strategic and important one, we should discuss it in more detail, it being the basis of the struggle to establish a government for the millions of Muslims on the earth. It is essential that those involved in the international Islamic movement observe peaceful means as peace leads to rallying the people and then it brings about and end to the obduracy of the enemy. Hence Imam Amir-ul-Mu'mineen (A) said: '*I would hate for you to become revilers.*' Before this the Holy Qur'an had said: **{And do not curse those who call upon other than Allah lest they curse Allah out of enmity and unwittingly.}** (6:108)

Cursing and enmity bring about loathing amongst friends and empower the enemy and there is no call for this. Arbitrary cursing ends up nowhere and what a person should be mindful of in front of his enemy is that he should seek to repel him with what is best as is found in the Holy Qur'an:

{Repel (evil) with that which is best for then you will find that your former enemy will become your warmest ally. But none shall achieve this but the patient ones and none shall achieve this except one blessed with great fortune.} (41:34-35)

So those involved in the Islamic movement should adopt peace in their thoughts, words, writings and confrontations and even if they organise demonstrations and strikes they should be characterised by calmness for what is important is to reach the goal and not an outpouring of hatred and loathing. For hatred only breeds hatred and loathing only breeds loathing. In the well-known aphorism: 'Grapes are not harvested from thorns.' Everything bears fruit of its own kind and good behaviour in a person brings about good behaviour in the person being dealt with. Bad behaviour only brings about a negative reaction. This applies equally to peace and its concomitants; each of them breeds its like.

This requires a degree of self-control and open-heartedness as Imam 'Ali (A) said: 'The tool of leadership is open-heartedness.' Meaning that your heart should remain open in all aspects – ethically and socially, intellectually, and in struggles, for this is the tool of leadership and the more this occurs, the more people will become attracted to the movement and the nearer it will take them to the desired objective.

Hence we can see that the phenomenon of good morals; forgiveness, peace, open-heartedness, kindness, humility, patience, not retaliating in the same way, but responding in the nicest way, appears in the lives of the all the great Prophets of Allah and the Impeccable Imams (A) and the great reformers. We see Imam Amir-ul-Mu'mineen (A) in the war of Basra (The battle of the Jamal), which was the first war to be waged against him, when the fighting had finished, Imam 'Ali strengthened the side of peace and sent a messenger to 'Aisha[56] saying she should return to her house in Madinah in peace. The Imam actually also clothed forty women in the clothes of men and sent them with 'Aisha to take her back to Madinah with her honour intact. They had donned the clothes of men for the reason that passing caravans would think that they were men and not attack them. Also 'Aisha, being the wife of the Prophet (S), Amir-ul-Mu'mineen (A) was loath to send her with men but preferred to send her with women. And indeed, 'Aisha went to Madinah from Basra in the company of these women. This is truly an example of the highest of morals.

We can also see that Imam 'Ali (A) forgave those who had stirred up the war with him even when there were amongst them those who would come under the category of war criminals in the modern terminology - the likes of Marwan and Ibn Zubeir who he pardoned. He also pardoned the opposing army saying: 'I grant to the people of Basra what the

[56] 'Aisha had led a war against Imam 'Ali, which became known as the War of Jamal.

Messenger of Allah (S) granted to the people of Mecca.' And he set them at liberty and did not take revenge of them and did not return their evil with evil but rather returned it with pardoning and kindness and he ordered that all the belongings that had been taken as spoils from the defeated army be returned. Everything was returned, even a cooking pot that had been taken and was being used to cook some broth was emptied of broth and returned. One time the Imam went on a reconnaissance mission to a grand house. He was told that women had gathered in it and were bewailing their dead soldiers from the defeated army and were cursing the Imam and his army. The Imam entered the house which was very large and full of the wives of the defeated army. The Imam said to his companions: 'Do not touch them even if they curse your manhood and your honour.' So he withheld his hands from them and replied to their curses with kindness. When they saw the Imam they began to shriek: 'This is the murderer of our beloveds!' Meaning Imam 'Ali (A). The Imam gestured and said: 'If I was the killer of your beloveds I would have killed those who are in these rooms (pointing to the rooms).' At once the women fell silent and did not say a word. The people were amazed at this and wondered what the Imam had said that had silenced the women. Later on the matter was disclosed to the companions of Imam 'Ali (A) that the leaders of the defeated army had hidden in those rooms and the women had gathered there as a ruse to cover up for them and to distract attention from them. So when the Imam pointed and said if I was the killer of your beloveds I would have killed those who are in these rooms they fell silent.

The life of the Prophet (S) and the life of Imam 'Ali (A) and the lives of the other Imams and great Prophets and the great reformers and great minds are summed up in the word 'peace'

Hence the world Islamic movement must observe peace in all its affairs before, during and after action and on the occasion of victory and establishing the Islamic state by the leave of Allah Almighty. The leaders should also educate the individuals in the Islamic movement about peace in the spoken word, thought, writing and action whatever the cost.

Peace Safeguards Islam

Allah Almighty is He says in the Qur'an: **{O you who have faith, enter into a state of peace one and all.}** (2:208)

Peace then is the general principle whereas violence is the exception, and exceptions are taken at face value. In the previous chapters we have mentioned the peaceful treatment by the Messenger of Allah (S) with his enemies and friends, his relatives and with strangers, and also that of Imam 'Ali (A). The Messenger of Allah and Imam 'Ali (S) are models for us as are the rest of the prophets and infallibles. Hence we should follow their lead whether we are in the beginnings of government or we have actually achieved government by the leave of Allah.

A question has been raised here: The Messenger of Allah (S) although he was infallible and will not be questioned about his actions, our task is not like his task. We see that he spared many hypocrites which led to many problems being caused for the Messenger of Allah. Had he killed Abu Sufyan and Mu'awiya on the day of the conquest of Mecca then the Umayyad state which ditched Islam completely would not have been formed, and it would not have caused the innumerable problems for the Muslims. Similarly, if Imam 'Ali had killed Marwan on the day of Basra, then he would not have been able to assume power and cause along with his descendants many problems. Therefore the point is made that we should adopt another task, while we should be aware of their conducts, but as far as their conducts is concerned they know what they are doing. This idea is refuted. Firstly, because the Prophet and the Imam are models, and the model should be followed whether we understand the reasoning behind their actions or not.

The Qur'anic verse says: **{And not a messenger have we sent except that he be obeyed by the leave of Allah.}** (4:64)

and in another verse: **{What the Messenger brings you then adopt it and what he forbids you then leave it.}** (59:7)

and in another verse: **{No by your Lord, they will not truly believe until they adopt you (the Messenger) as a judge in those matters in which they disagree amongst themselves, then do not find in themselves any complaint about your judgements and they submit completely.}** (4:65)

This is from the point of view of belief and Divine Law. From the point of view of the intellect, we believe that had the Messenger of Allah (S) killed Abu Sufyan and his like then Islam would not have been supported nor would it have taken root and sprouted because the Polytheists would have buried Islam in its cradle. Abu Sufyan was not alone. In the Arabian Peninsula there were a thousand Abu Sufyans and each of then had relatives, friends, family, and clan. They would have buried Islam in its cradle and we would not even hear any mention today of the Messenger of Allah (S) in the same way that we do not hear about many of the other prophets of Allah who were killed. The Qur'anic verse says: **{Then why do you kill the prophets of Allah if you have faith}** (2:91) and this shows that many prophets were killed.

The Messenger of Allah Muhammad (S) was faced with a choice between leaving the hypocrites who, if they caused a few problems would be effaced by time eventually as time has effaced the Umayyad clan and consigned them to the mists of history, or the other choice of raising his sword and killing and killing until the tribes arose and killed him and his loyal companions leaving no trace of Islam left.

The same applies to Imam 'Ali (A). Was he to unsheathe his sword and kill them and face the consequences of their tribes and relatives and friends moving against him helped by the Romans, and by this uprooting Imam 'Ali (A) which meant uprooting Islam itself and it being changed into a corrupt religion like Judaism and Christianity as the Qur'anic verse says: **{And they change the words from their rightful places.}**. (5:13)

Or was it better to spare those people who if they denigrated Islam it would only be for a short time.

This then was the plan of the Messenger and Imam 'Ali, a very wise plan indeed. Hence we find that one of the companions of Imam 'Ali (A) describe him as being: 'Farsighted and with powerful faculties.' We see Imam 'Ali (A) now after almost 1400 years since his martyrdom has more than 1000 million people believing in him, Muslim and non-Muslim alike. Whereas the Umayyads and the 'Abbasids have been consigned to the mists of time and are only mentioned with disdain. So the Messenger of Allah (S) remains and those who opposed him like Abu Jahl, Abu Sufyan, and Abu Lahab were destroyed. One of the benefits of peace is that the memory of the peace-maker remains as do his laws, checks and balances and methods whereas memory of the non-peace-maker does not remain even if it is assumed that he was one-hundred percent right. Hence the Messenger of Allah (S) said:

'*Whenever the Angel Gabriel descended upon me he ordered me to maintain good relations with people.*'

In recent history, we see that Stalin and Hitler and Mussolini and the like inclined to violence as did Yasin al-Hashimi in Iraq, Pahlevi in Iran and Ataturk in Turkey and there are many others like them and all of them have gone. Stalin was exhumed and his corpse burned and all the Stalinist principles destroyed. As for Hitler, up until recently his country was split between the Americans and the Russians. Mussolini's country was in chaos and disruption and the 'Red Brigades' was widespread as was murder, assassination, and theft for more than forty years. The first Pahlevi was expelled and assassinated in Mauritius. Yasin al-Hashemi was expelled from Iraq and killed, and Ataturk was killed.

In addition to these people becoming the accursed of history, they have vanished, as have their principles. History only regards them now as a lesson to be learned from as Pharaoh, Shidad, and Nimrod became lessons, and also Mu'awiya, Yazid, al-Hajjaj, Ibn Ziyad, and Harun. Those who come after them may learn from them not to incline to dictatorship and violence but rather to right thinking, decisiveness and peace, and conferring freedoms, and looking towards the people with the eye of friendship and brotherhood even if they were infidels. As Imam 'Ali (A) said: '*People are of two types; Either your brother in religion or your equal in creation.*'

Allah Exalted is He, in the Qur'an speaks about the believers and the non-believers being brothers when he says: **{And to the people of 'Ad we sent their brother Salih.}** (6:65). Salih is a messenger and prophet whose tribe 'Ad were infidels but Allah still calls him their brother.

The important thing for the people concerned with the Islamic movement is to be aware of this reality of brotherhood and to remain patient and to pay attention to the previous nations. **{Say, Travel throughout the land . . .}** (16:69, 29:20, 30:42), **{Walk in the uplands of the earth and eat of what He provides you with . . .}** (67:15). One must look and think about the previous nations and the state of modern nations.

Those who incline to peace remain well known in their own lands and elsewhere whereas those who tend to violence and coarseness and force if they are known at all are despised and disowned.

Allah says regarding His Prophet: **{By the mercy of Allah, you were mild mannered with them. Had you been ill mannered and hard hearted they would have deserted you.}** (3:159)

If we adopt peacefulness as a practical principle always, we will, by the leave of Allah, be able to initiate a general trend towards an authentic Islamic movement which will be a prelude to rescuing the Islamic lands from the colonialists and dictators and to establish the law of Allah for one billion Muslims. For Allah this is not difficult.

Peace Amongst Members of the Movement

We have discussed the principle of peace from a number of viewpoints including peaceful social interaction and peaceful interaction with the enemy. Now we will discuss the same principle but from another angle namely the peaceful interaction amongst the members of the Islamic movement itself. This means that the members of the movement should be in complete accord and there should not be any differences or disputes. Often there occurs amongst the members of an organisation unhealthy competition and wrangling and disputes and mutual hatreds. This problem has two bases:

The first is that some people seek to exploit others and the second is that those people of higher rank look to the lower ranking members with disgust and the lower ranking member look to the higher ranking members as exploitative and arrivists and opportunists. Islam provides solution to both of these problems:

The decision making process must be that of mutual consultation (*Shura*) so that every individual has an opinion which must be considered. By this, exploitation leading to the break-up and death of the movement will cease. As for he who says: I have a greater understanding, or my vision of the future is deeper so I have the right to decide in the matter, this is exactly what is meant by exploitation. This will solve the first problem.

As for the second problem, people should not have contempt for one another or belittle one another. **{O you who believe, avoid suspicion, for some suspicion is a crime.}** (49:12)

Suspicions must be avoided. Imam Amir-ul-Mu'mineen (A) said: *'Give your brother the benefit of the doubt'*, and in another tradition from Imam al-Saadiq (A) who said: *'If fifty people swear to you that he said something and he says that he did not say it then believe him and do not believe them.'* Meaning that do not doubt him on the basis of what those traitors say.

One of the impeccable Imams (A) visited one of the Caliphs during an emergency situation. The Caliph said to the Imam: *'O son of the*

Messenger of Allah (S), advise me.' The Imam (A) said: *'The Muslims are either older than you in which case you should treat them as you would your father. Or they are younger than you in which case you should treat them as you would your son. Or they are equal to you in age in which case you should treat them as you would treat your brother. Honour your father, treat your brother equally and have mercy upon your son.'* This is the way a person should look towards everyone; with kindness and mercy, sympathy and compassion and if not then he will not be able to progress however powerful he is. These are the foundations upon which the Messenger of Allah (S) built the Islamic state and upon which the impeccable Imams built the personalities of the Muslim believers.

It is related that Imam al-Saadiq (A) went to Karbala to visit the grave of Imam al-Hussein (A) and he said to one of his companions: *'Go around and invite whoever you see to visit Imam al-Hussein (A).' The man went but returned without anyone. The Imam said to him: 'Why have you returned alone?' The man said: 'O son of the Messenger of Allah, I didn't think the people I met were good enough.' The Imam said to him: 'Then I think of you what you think of them.'* Meaning that if there is a difference in the levels of people then the difference between you and them is the same as the difference between myself and you, and as it is not right for the higher ranking person to reject the middle ranking person, it is also not right for the middle ranking person to reject the lower ranking person.

In the same way, there should be a state of harmony and peace amongst those involved with the Islamic movement, and not a state of exploitation, antipathy, and contempt.

The Islamic movement will not be able to guide the people to the straight path as long as it itself does not follow the straight path. There is a well-known principle in reasoning that says: 'That which lacks something cannot bestow that thing.' If you do not have knowledge how can you bestow knowledge? If you do not own a Dinar how can you give away a Dinar? Similarly, if the building blocks of the Islamic movement are not equality, justice, the love of people, and humility it will not be able to plant these things in other people. It is just not possible.

Those involved in the Islamic movement therefore should look to one another with equality, fraternity and justice so that they might progress by the leave of Allah. If not then the people will say: If there were any good in their movement they themselves would have adopted what they were calling for.

Many Islamic movements have failed in the past because of a failure to adopt the ethics of action and peace. These failed movements should be a lesson to us so that we act in a way that will make the movement righteous so we can achieve, by the leave of Allah, the international Islamic state of more than one billion Muslims.

The Results of Peace

Peace results in the best outcome. Those who make peace remain, however many enemies they have. Even if they stumble and fall it will only be temporary. Those involved in the Islamic movement if they surround themselves with an air of peace they will firstly halt their enemies and they will not be able to destroy them, and secondly, if their enemy is able to get to them this will only be temporary and will eventually end in advancement for the peace-makers.

We can see that the Prophets and Imams (A) always inclined to peace. The Messenger of Allah (S) used to make peace with his enemies even when he was at the height of his power and his wars were all defensive in nature as history shows. The Messenger of Allah (S) did not initiate a single war ever and if he did do battle, his battles were characterised by peace except to the amount that was necessary. Because of this the Messenger of Allah (S) made great advances and still does to this very day. Not a day goes by but the number of Muslims increases despite what the Islamic state has had to face in the way of plots and ploys from the first day of its existence until now.

Also Imam 'Ali (A) inclined to peace to the utmost of his capacity. He did not make war on the people of the Jamal but they made war on him and solely because the war ended he dealt with those who remained as if they were friends and brothers and as if nothing had happened. This was also the case with the battle of Nahrawan where the Kharijites had made war against the Imam and spread rumours and insulted him until the Imam made a beautiful speech (to be found in *Nahj al-Balagha*) while around him were his companions. A Kharijite heard the speech and commented on it saying: 'Allah curse him for his infidelity how wise he is.' Meaning that Imam 'Ali is an infidel but he is wise. His companions wanted to punish the Kharijite but the Imam said: 'Leave him for the rule is a curse for a curse or forgiveness of sin and I prefer to forgive.' Meaning that he has cursed me so I am entitled to curse him back or forgive and I am more worthy of the second so he pardoned him. In fact Imam 'Ali (A) was able to gain control over the Kharijite movement which was a corrupt movement with his calmness and flexibility.

The chronicles show that when the war with the Kharijites had ended, the Imam (A) forgave what remained of them and did not imprison them or punish them in any other way. They were in Kufa and elsewhere denigrating the Imam (A) but he remained silent for he knew that the peace-maker will eventually make progress. The Kharijites were making life difficult for the Imam in many ways like attending the mosque but not praying with him the congregational prayer. Once a Kharijite read the following Qur'anic verse in front of the Imam: **{And it was revealed to you and to those before you that if you associate partners with Allah your actions will be in vain.}** (39:65). Implying by this that the Imam (A) was a *Mushrik* (one who associates partners with Allah) and that his actions were in vain. Still the Imam pardoned him. This was the nature of the Imam; patient in the face of criticism even oppressive criticism, and patient in the face of pressure even if this pressure came from corrupt people for he knew that peace provides the most noble consequences and that the peace-maker survives as we indeed see ourselves that he has survived for 1400 years and he will survive until the end of history no matter what the circumstances.

In the battle of Siffin, one of the most violent battles against the Imam (A) the chronicles report that when the Imam defeated a soldier from the army of Mu'awiya he would ask him to swear not to assist Mu'awiya again then he would leave him to his own devices. This is unheard of in history except in the history of the Imams and the Prophets and the great reformers who followed their footsteps.

Because of this, we see that the Imam (A) has remained like a lofty mountain despite the fact that the Umayyad Clan put pressure upon him and cursed him from seventy thousand pulpits for almost one-hundred years, and despite the fact that the 'Abbasid Clan oppressed him including the Caliph Mutawakkil who made war upon him and killed his sons and imprisoned them and desecrated the grave of Hussein (A) and destroyed Karbala twice as is to be found in the chronicles. A man called 'Ubadah al-Mukhnath used to come to meetings and put a pillow between his shirt and stomach and walk around the gathering saying: "I am Amir-ul-Mu'mineen." Making fun of Imam 'Ali (A) while everyone present laughed.

But what was the outcome? Those people only hurt themselves and not the Imam except superficially. The Imam (A) said once: '*I have not been kind to anyone and no-one has harmed me.' Those around him said: 'O Commander of the Faithful, you have been kind to many and many have harmed you.' He said: 'Have you not heard Allah's words:* ***{If you do good you do it to yourselves and if you do harm then you do it against yourselves.}***[57]*, for I have done good to myself by doing good to others and the people have done ill to themselves by doing ill to me.*'

In fact, those who put pressure upon the Imam (A) from the Umayyad and Abbasid Clans and their ilk only injured themselves. Mutawakkil was killed along with his vizier al-Fath ibn al-Khaqan as were those who came before him and after him. The Imam remains like a lofty mountain, or a shining sun that illuminates more than one billion people on earth.

All of this was due to the nature of the movement of the Imam (A) and his peacefulness that he adopted as a motto in his personal, family, and social life.

The *hadith* reports that Ibn Muljim, when he struck the Imam (A), the Imam said to him: '*Have I not been good to you, did I not give to you generously?*' The Imam despite having knowledge given to him by the Messenger of Allah (S) that Ibn Muljim would kill him, he continued to favour him and treat him kindly. After Ibn Muljim had struck by his sword on his head, Imam Ali still ordered that he be treated well. When he drank milk he would leave some and say: '*Feed your prisoner.*' The Imam had also said to his sons: '*If I recover from this blow of his I will pardon him. If I do not recover then you have the right of retaliation but do not mutilate the man for I heard the Messenger of Allah (S) saying: 'Do not mutilate even a rabid dog.*' However he recommended that his sons pardon the man.

Likewise, Mu'awiya has gone and the Kharijites have perished and the people of the Jamal have passed away as have Haroun and Mutawakkil and Ma'moun and others like them who used to oppose the Imam (A). They have all gone and the Imam remains as a minaret illuminating travellers.

The Islamic movement which seeks a resurgence in order to establish the government of a billion Muslims must also adopt peace as its watchword

---

[57] *The Holy Qur'an:* The Ascension (17): 7.

so that it might be able to attract the people and repel the enemy. And if the Islamic movement were to stumble and fall then it would inevitably arise again. And because it is human nature to support peace-makers and to exact revenge upon the war makers, then if the Islamic movement adopts peace as its mantra properly and not just as an empty slogan, in word, deed, thought, writing, speech, and in gatherings then it will be able to expand until it encompasses all the lands of Islam. This will be the beginning of the government of a billion Muslims by the leave of Allah.

Equilibrium of Thought and Deed Results in Peace

Peace cannot happen, nor can it be realised in the external reality unless the thought-processes and actions of the human being are in equilibrium and far from guesses and arbitrariness, exaggerations and negligence.

If a person sees in himself and his group all the good and virtue, and sees others as being devoid of virtue and immersed in vice, this type of thinking will only lead to other than peace, to enmity and hatred, attacks and innuendo. It is well known that there are three things, a little of which is considered great; fire, enmity, and illness. A single match can set light to a whole timber store of tens of tons of wood. A small illness can lead to death. A minor enmity like a nasty word can lead to bloodshed.

The chroniclers have reported that the war of the *Busus*, which lasted around one hundred years, began when a man from one tribe shot an arrow into the side of a camel of another tribe. The owner of the camel killed the man who had shot the arrow whose family killed the owner of the camel and so on and so forth. The poet has said: *Most of the fire is made of mere sparks.*

Hence it is imperative that a person thinks in a balanced way so that balanced actions will result from it. If he were to think in an exaggerated manner, then this will only result in corrupt action and from there to enmity and hatred.

If a person wishes to undertake an international Islamic movement resulting in the government of one billion Muslims then he must adopt peace as his watchword in his speech, action, writing, and movement. The prophet Jesus (A) alluded to this when he said: '*When someone strikes your right cheek then turn the left cheek to him.*'

Jesus does not mean by this that the oppressed should submit to the oppressors but rather he means something else which the Holy Qur'an also points to in the verse: **{ . . . but to pardon is closer to piety.}** (2:237). Jesus wanted success for his followers and to attract the people. Therefore he taught them peace to this extent. Jesus was successful in this and we can see that more than two billion people in the world today respect him, half of whom are Christians and the other half Muslims.

In another piece of wisdom related about the Messiah (A) is that he and a group of his disciples passed by a group of Jews who said some unkind words to him. He replied with kind words. Naturally he spoke the truth when he spoke good about them as most evil people have at least some aspect of good in them. He was asked: '*Why do you speak kindly of them when the speak unkindly of you.' He said: 'Each person spends of that which he owns.*' Meaning that whoever harbours evil will speak in evil terms and *vice versa.* One who owns a dinar may give away that dinar whereas one who has nothing but a poisonous scorpion can only give away a scorpion.

This is also the case with one who harbours good or evil. The faculties of hearing sight, and writing and the like if they emanate from a heart full of goodness and mercy, then these faculties will be characterised by goodness and mercy. The opposite is also the case. If the heart is full of evil and lies, then the tongue and the rest of the faculties will only be able to express what is in that heart. This is what Jesus (A) teaches us; if the other party is not good then at least be good yourself.

In the supplication for the month of Rajab are the words: '*O He who I beg of him for every good and seek sanctuary from His displeasure for every evil. O He who gives much in exchange for little. O He who gives to he who asks Him and he who does not ask Him or know Him, out of his kindness and mercy.'*

Allah gives to the believers and also to those who do not know Him or oppose Him. He gives even to those who oppose Him. The Holy Qur'an alludes to this in the verse: **{Nay We will provide for those people and those from the gift of your Lord.}** (17:20)

If we wish to adopt the ethics of Allah Almighty, then we must be balanced in thought and in deed and not raise our friends to the highest heaven and neglect those who are impartial. Everything should be in equilibrium. Among the benefits of a person who is in equilibrium in his thoughts and actions is that people will approve of his judgements and will join his camp. However this is something that requires self-control and the ability to bear criticisms, which are difficult matters, but out of difficulties a good result can arise.

In a *hadith* from the Messenger of Allah (S) that when he saw Fatima (A) toiling and tiring herself he said: '*Take now the bitterness of this world for the sweetness of the next.*' Bitter things only produce a sweet outcome.

Any engineer, doctor, lawyer, sportsman, or gifted speaker or writer will not have reached his station except through hard work and toil. So must we if we want to reach the goal of a government of one billion Muslims.

This requires self-control and a balance in thought and the capacity to bear criticism and the ability to convince people without any despotic or dictatorial means. Despotism and dictatorship, and extremism in thought, word and deed, and in the administrative system will only result in bad consequences.

There is a *hadith* that Jesus (A) passed by a murdered person and he said: '*Who killed you?, there will come a day when they will kill your killer.*' This is almost a natural law, that the person who kills another will see a day in which he himself will be killed. In another *hadith* come the words: '*Give the killer tidings that he will be killed and the adulterer that he will be poor.*'

One of the conditions of the international Islamic movement is that it should adopt peace from the viewpoint of equilibrium in thought and deed and giving everything its due. In the Holy Qur'an: {**. . . and do not withhold from the people their belongings.**} (7:85, 11:85, 26:183)

This means that if you write a book and praise yourself for doing so and someone else writes ten good books and you do not praise him to the amount of your book then this will result in you being left behind in life in addition to the fact that the people will desert you and will know you for being immodest.

Hence it is well known amongst our scholars that a source of religious knowledge or the Imam of a congregation or the judge must distance themselves from arbitrary love and hate.

We have previously mentioned that a man said to Shaikh Murtada al-Ansari: '*It is easy for a human being to become a scholar, but it is impossible for him to become a human being.*' Meaning by this that you the Sheikh are a scholar and this is something easy but you are not a human being and that this is impossible for you to achieve. The Sheikh said: '*On the contrary, for a human being to become a scholar is difficult and for him to become a human being is even more difficult.*'

This is true, for a person must strive for fifty or sixty years day and night in order to become a scholar. If he wants to become a human being then his striving must be deeper in order to achieve his goal.

Building Blocks of Peace Within the Movement

To have peace within the Islamic movement requires the presence of two things without which the movement will not end with a good result but will remain weak and ineffective as have many movements in the past who have come to the fore then disappeared because they did not have realistic building blocks for the movement. This applies to both the Islamic and non-Islamic worlds. Hence the Islamic movement should observe these two matters from the initial stages of its formation so that it may reach the desired goal. These two matters are:

Firstly: Free and fair elections within the movement itself and a balance of power. Naturally splits will form in the movement. This is customary in life. However between these splits there must be equality, balance and competence so that a single group is not able to take control of the movement and derail the movement towards dictatorship. Any movement can be taken from reality to dictatorship simply by one group gaining authority over the other groups. This spells death for the movement even if the movement remains alive superficially.

Before the western military coups in Iraq and although British colonialism was in authority at that time, it was not as powerful and sharp as the colonialism that those who called themselves republicans brought. They were not in fact republicans, not al-Karim, nor al-Salaam, nor his brother, nor al-Bakr, nor those who came after him. They were nothing but agents of Britain, Israel and America. In any case, at the time of the monarchy, many political parties whether they called themselves the National Party or the Progressive Party, or even the Islamic Party, all failed for the reason that at the very beginning a colonialist or despotic group gained control over them and there were no free elections, equalities or distribution of power. This should be a lesson to us. The Islamic movement must have power bases within it, which are both equal and competitive, but the competition should be towards the good and not the bad, towards decisive action and attracting the people and raising standards. As Allah has said in three verses from the Holy Qur'an: **{ . . . and for this let the competitors compete for.}** (3:133), and { . . . **and race each other for forgiveness from your Lord.**} (2:148), and { . . . **and race for the good things.**} (5:48).

Whatever the case may be, it is imperative that the Islamic movement should observe peace between the different groups of the movement and if dictatorship should gain power over the movement then there will be no peace, for peace is bred from equal power bases. If dictatorship were to gain power it would not change and the movement would not be able to change it. Then this group would act despotically with the finances, the reputation of the movement and with the will of the movement. We have seen how easy it was for colonialism to take the reins of power from the dictators because the public was taken out of the equation and the power was present in four, five or ten people only. However, if the movement had been a popular movement then colonialism would not have been able to take the reins of power from the people.

It is then imperative that the movement observe the following two points. First, the movement should comprise of different branches, equally balanced powers, and different groups each with their own currents and trends even though the framework is one, which is the popular Islamic movement. It is only natural that people's tastes are different and each person should be allowed to propose his own opinion in a climate of complete freedom be that in speech, writing, in gatherings or on travels. Every person should work according to his own opinion as we see in action amongst religious jurists. Their framework is the Qur'an and the Sunnah, consensus and intellect but they still differ in the particularities in all the areas of jurisprudence. This is the case for doctors, engineers, and astronomers in the gatherings of the free or semi-free nations.

Secondly, the movement should also hold free elections annually or biennially. The mark of free elections is a complete change from top to bottom not fraudulent elections as in some nations, parties and organisations where the leaders do not change and only a few things change as a tactic. Another mark of fair elections is that the number of votes ranges from small to large like 51% or 55% or 60%. As for forged elections like those of the Ba'thists or the Nationalists we see 99% of the votes going to the former president and 1% going to his opponent or even less. This is nothing but fraud, lies, and does nothing but compound the dictatorship. A political scientist has laid down two criteria for assessing whether a country is free or not. The first is to see whether the leaders change once every four years. The second is to see whether the people are able to speak freely in the streets or write what they wish or publish magazines and newspapers as they wish. These two criteria must be observed within the movement itself so that the movement can be fully free on the condition that this freedom be within an Islamic framework.

Through this, the movement may be able to continue to expand and progress and will be accompanied by peace. In this way the movement will end in the government of one billion Muslims by the leave of Allah.

Instilling Peace

The process of instilling and instructing the self has a great effect on the human psyche. Humans are by nature prone to anger and revolt, to seeing the faults of others, to entering into wrangles and fights with others, and to hatred, disdain, enmity and cutting off relationships. It is imperative that the roots of these things are extirpated from the heart of the individual and following on from that the rest of his limbs. This can be achieved through instilling into the self that the human being is a harmoniser, a peace-maker, decisive, intelligent, a thinking being, a purposeful being, and an administrator. If the individual instils this into his self day and night and throughout his life he will eventually develop a peaceful nature and he will be able to help to advance the Islamic movement even in an environment of wars, revolts and revolutions.

In a *hadith* it is said: '*The most worthy of things to be imprisoned is the tongue.*' Hence the individual must customise himself to guarding his tongue and his heart.

In another *hadith* it is said: '*If you see the believer silent then draw near to him for he is receiving wisdom.*'

The individual must also guard his hand and his pen, his movements and his pauses in fact everything so that he may move the Islamic nation forward. Those who say: 'We are nervous characters and we cannot bear pressure', or they say: 'So-and-So has belittled our opinion', or they say: 'We think he is in the wrong so how can we remain silent?' These types of people are not able to advance the movement.

Hence we see in the history of the Messenger of Allah (S) and the history of successful movements many of this type of person. The *hadith* report that an ill-mannered man of the infidels came to the Messenger of Allah (S) and cursed him while the Messenger was in the sacred mosque reciting the Qur'an. The Messenger of Allah did not say a word to him but the man obviously wanted to provoke a fight with the Messenger of

Allah (S). The Messenger remained calm and quiet but the man cursed him and cursed him. Then he spat in the face of the Messenger of Allah (S). The man himself continues the account saying that: 'Muhammad (S) did no more than wipe the spit off his face and did not say a thing.' What was it that made the Messenger of Allah do this when he was justified in at least returning what he had received with like as in the Qur'anic verse: **{. . . and whoever attacks you then attack them in the same way that they attack you.}** (2:194). It was because the Messenger of Allah (S) saw that entering into a squabble with this infidel was not important and it would not serve his goal. Hence he returned to peace and carried on in the way that Allah had marked out for him. In this way the Islamic movement succeeded because of the clemency, patience and peacefulness of the Messenger of Allah (S). The poet says: '*You will never be able to be clement until you adopt clemency.*' Meaning that if there is revolution in your heart then do not let it surface but rather adopt clemency and patience and control yourself so that you are able to be a peace-maker even in the worst times of excitement and breakdown.

There is another account about the Messenger of Allah (S) that he passed by the family of Yasir; Yasir and Sumayyah and 'Ammar, when the Polytheists were torturing them. He looked at them with kindness and said: '*Patience O family of Yasir for you have been promised paradise.*' He did no more than this. This was because the Messenger of Allah (S) knew that if he entered into a marginal dispute with the torturers he would lose his main impetus and he would not reach his main goal, which was to establish the pillars of Islam. In this way, the Messenger, his righteous companions and his impeccable family were characterised with the most amount of peacefulness and peace, self control and control of the tongue, hand and reaction. They were then able to make advances because of this peace.

We can also see that some reformers who were able to rescue their countries from the grip of colonialism were able to control themselves. One who was not able to do this and would get irritated at the slightest thing began to instil in himself every day the qualities of a peace-maker who loves the good for all people. He used to say: 'Every day when I awoke in the morning I would instil these things in myself and also when I wanted to sleep until I was able to carry pressure and insults.'

The Muslim instils in himself peace every morning, noon, afternoon, at sunset, and evening in the obligatory prayers when he repeats in every prayer: '*Peace be upon you O Prophet and the Blessings and Mercy of Allah, Peace be upon you O righteous servants of Allah, Peace be upon you and the blessings and mercy of Allah.'* Peace to the leader namely the Messenger of Allah (S), peace to himself and peace for everyone else. This symbolises the peacefulness of the leader, the peacefulness of the person, and the peacefulness of the Islamic community or greater than the Islamic community because saying 'Peace be upon you' encompasses everyone to enter into peace. In this way the Muslim instils peace into himself every day at least fifteen times. If the individual instils peacefulness into himself he will have the peace which will enable him to lead, to progress, to bear difficulties, not to become irritated with others through insulting words or slander and backbiting and cursing. There is a *hadith* in which the Messenger of Allah saw two people cursing each other so he said: '*They are two Satans reviling each other.'*

Whatever the case may be, the Islamic movement which seeks to bring about an international Islamic government must adopt peace as its mantra, and strive for peace. Not the peace of the communists for this is the peace of infidelity and killing. What we seek is an Islam in the shade of Peace meaning in the shade of Allah for one of His names is al-Salam (Peace):

{He is Allah, there is no god but He, The King, The Holy, The Peace, The Faithful, The Protector, The Almighty, The Omnipotent, The Imperious.} (59:23)

What we seek is a peace in the shade of peace, which is in the shade of Allah and in the shade of Islam. Hence we should always try to instil in ourselves peace and compassion, even for the enemy, so that we may draw them to the straight path. It has been related that the Messenger of Allah (S) if the harm he suffered from his people became great would say: '*O Allah, guide my people, for they have no knowledge.'* He did not seek to invoke Allah against them but rather called upon Allah to guide them. In the end the Messenger of Allah achieved that success which has no parallel in the entire world. We ask Allah to grant us such success in this. Surely He is the granter of success and the best helper.

Part Three

In this paper the author addresses the issue of non-violence as prescribed in the teachings of Islam; that violence is severely condemned and non-violence is encouraged. The author then goes on to classify violence, and non-violence, into three categories. The author shows how non-violence produces the desired results in all aspects of life, and it is therefore incumbent for the Islamic reform movement to adhere to non-violence if they want to achieve reforms in their societies successfully.

This paper is an extract from Imam Shirazi's book, ***The Islamic Government***, pp 66-88, volume 102 of the "*Al-Fiqh* series.

Translated by Z. Olyabek

Non-Violence in the Teachings of Islam

One of the most important principles that the forthcoming Islamic government, as well as the Islamic movement, must adhere to is the condition of non-violence. A substantial body of the holy tradition and reports condemns violence as may be found in *"The Shi'a Guide to Shari'ah (Islamic Law)"*[58] and *"Supplement to The Shi'a Guide to the Shari'ah"*[59]. It is also reported *"Violence is also part of the army of ignorance"*. Furthermore, there is equally substantial evidence in the holy traditions and reports encouraging and promoting non-violence, leniency and kindness.

To show the correlation between violence and non-violence the following introduction is presented.

Ancient philosophers considered the universe to be composed of four elements; namely water, earth, fire and air. Furthermore all four elements were considered to be the derivatives of one entity called primordial matter. The four elements were considered to have interchangeable states, just as different shapes and structures can be made from clay whereas the basic substance, clay, remains the same.

Sociologists make similar statements in relation to power. To them power is an essence that may manifest itself in a tribe, wealth, knowledge, the nation state, or public opinion and so on, all of which may transform from one state to another. For example the tribal chief may transfer his power and influence to the domain of public opinion, and from there to the nation state. As seen in the case of an individual who gains power through the support and vote of public opinion.

The legislators state a similar argument regarding law and custom. They are both of the same essence, and one may be transmuted into the other and vice versa. For example if it was a custom to drive on the right hand side of the road, members of parliament are pressured to make that convention a law. On the other hand, if the traffic regulation states that cars must stop at the red traffic light, people would abide by that and it becomes common custom.

---

[58] Compiled by Hassan al-Hurr al-Aameli as *"Wasaa'el al-Shi'a le Tasheel Masaa'el al-Shari'ah"*.

[59] Compiled by Mirza Hussain al-Noori as *"Mostadrak al-Wasaa'el"*.

As for Islamic law, Allah states; ***"Allah will change their evil (deed) into good."***[60]

This is because the essence is one. Another example is the concept of the tree in heaven and in hell. They both are of the same essence but one gives dates and grapes and the other gives fire and fruits like the heads of demons. The example of this (transmutability) in this world is:

"Have you not seen those who have changed the favour of Allah into blasphemy?"[61] where grapes are turned into wine or, on the other hand, wine is turned into vinegar.

Having given this introduction I would state that violence and non-violence are of the same essence. They reflect the human will in repelling harm and attracting good, whether in wealth, honour, or the self. The human will may be released either through violence or non-violence and the latter is the desirable of the two options.

Therefore it is imperative upon Islamist activists and the Islamic government to opt for non-violence to reach their objectives, which are the establishment of the Islamic government, as far as the activists are concerned, or its survival as far the established government is concerned, so that it (the state) may expand and develop quantitively and qualitatively.

As for the kind of non-violence that must be adopted, it must be the kind adopted 'by nature' and not that adopted 'by coercion'. Non-violence may be categorised in three classes:

Non-violence by nature:

In this category an individual is by nature non-violent, just as he may have other character traits such as bravery, nobility, justness, chastity...

Non-violence by coercion:

This is a kind of non-violence that is adopted by an individual due to his weakness. The weak person resorts to non-violence

[60] The holy Qur'an: The Criterion (25): 70.
[61] The holy Qur'an: Abraham (14): 28.

to achieve his objectives. Therefore if a bullying tyrant slaps an individual in the face, the latter would not respond because he is unable to do so as he is no match to the former. This is the worst kind of non-violence. This is similar to the case of one who refrains from swearing back since he is dumb.

Non-violence by design:

In this case non-violence is adopted in preference to violence on the basis of priorities. In this case one is able to resort to violence, unlike the one in the second kind above, but non-violence is not his 'second nature' as in the first case. Here non-violence is preferred over violence since it serves as a strategy to achieve his objectives.

It may be argued that the second category should not be called non-violence as it is not applicable! For example, can we say that an infant baby who is unable to respond back if hit is a case of non-violence?

The answer would be that this is not what it is meant by the second category. What is meant is the capacity for violence, where the use of violence would bring about the downfall of one's aims. For example swearing at someone who had slapped him or slapping someone who had shot him.

Just as non-violence is defined in three categories, violence is also classified in three categories, according to the law of pairs. And given that the probability that nonentity is one, therefore there cannot be several nonentities versus many existences, absolute existence is opposed by absolute nihility. As for external existences, they are opposed by specific nihility. Therefore the existence of X is opposed by the non-existence of X, but not opposed by absolute nihility. Just as absolute existence is opposed by absolute nihility and not the non-existence of X. Either of the two absolutes have respective entities; just as they (the absolutes) oppose one another, their entities do too. Needless to say, two opposing entities should be equal in every aspect except in existence and non-existence. Therefore the existence of X is not opposed by the non-existence of Y. This is a philosophical debate that is beyond the scope of this writing.

The purpose of this debate is that it is imperative for the Islamic movement and government to be characterised by non-violence of the first category, i.e. *non-violence by nature*. This is because in addition to reaching the pleasant goal that will be characterised by continual existence, non-violence is a virtue that comforts the soul too. And what a difference there is between one who does something or refrains from something willingly and one who does so reluctantly.

It may be asked, "If this is the case, then why do we see that the prophets and imams engaged in violence, as stated in the Qur'an?

"How many of the Prophets fought (in Allah's way), and with them (fought) large bands of godly men?"[62] and

"O Prophet! Fight the Unbelievers and the Hypocrites, . . ."[63],

And why did the imams Ali, Hassan and Hussain (A) participate in wars?" The reply to this is that this was based on a question of priorities. The issue was to choose the lesser of two evils; just as when a patient reluctantly agrees to undergo a surgical operation to amputate a limb in order to prevent greater harm to his body and health. If the Messenger of Allah, (S), had ignored the pagans and their mischievous deeds and had left them to their own accords, that would have resulted in the loss of thousands, if not millions, of lives, whereas the given response of the Messenger of Allah (S) limited it to less than fourteen hundred.[64] So on the one hand we have violence with tens of thousands or millions, and on the other violence with less than fourteen hundred. Clearly the latter would not be called violence compared to the first.

Acquiring a Non-violence Discipline

The virtue of non-violence requires a substantial and, very often, a strenuous psychological and character forming education and training.

"None shall be accorded this rank except one blessed with great good fortune."[65]

Non-violence has many manifestations. It is not merely to refrain from swearing back at someone who swore at you, or to abstain from hitting back at whoever hit you or shot you. To stubbornly hold on to your

---

[62] The holy Qur'an: The Family of 'Emran (3): 146.
[63] The holy Qur'an: Repentance (9): 73.
[64] This figure includes the casualties on both sides throughout the campaigns.
[65] The holy Qur'an: Well-Expounded (41): 35.

views when amongst a group who have opposite views to yours, refusing the majority opinion, is also a manifestation of violence. Stubbornness is a kind of violence. Another kind of violence is to frown at others, and another is to pass by someone without greeting him. All of these, amongst others, are manifestation of violence. Hence Islam actively encourages desirable behaviour and practices such as "making a bond with whoever severed with you, and giving generously to he who denied you". Examples of some of the reported traditions that encourage such virtues are as follows:

The Messenger of Allah (S) is quoted as saying, *"Shall I inform you of the best morals of this world and the hereafter? (They are) To forgive he who oppresses you, to make a bond with he who severs from you, to be kind to he who insults you, and to give to he who deprives you."*

Imam Zayn el-Abidin[66] (A) is quoted as saying: *"On the day of Judgement Allah the Almighty assembles all the people in one location and then it is announced, "Where are the noble people?" A group of people rise, who are then asked, "What distinguishes you from the rest?" In reply they say: "We used to make bonds with he who broke off with us, We used to give to he who deprived us, We used to forgive he who used to oppress us." They are then told; "You have said the truth, so enter the heaven."*

In another tradition, Imam Saadiq[67] (A) is reported as saying: *"Three noble qualities belong to this world and the hereafter: To forgive he who oppresses you, To make bonds with he who breaks off with you, To forbear when insulted."*

In another tradition Imam Baaqir[68] (A) is reported as saying: *"Allah the Almighty gives nothing but honour and esteem to the Muslim who has three qualities: Forgiving he who has oppressed him, Giving to he who has deprived him, and Making bonds with he who has severed links with him."*

In another tradition, Imam Ridha (A) quotes the Messenger of Allah (S) as saying: *"Let it be a duty upon you to observe the most noble of ethics,*

---

[66] Imam Zayn el-Aabedeen, also known as Imam al-Sajjad, is the fourth infallible imam of the Muslims after the Messenger of Allah (S).

[67] Imam Saadiq is the sixth infallible imam of the Muslims after the Messenger of Allah (S).

[68] Imam Baaqir is the fifth infallible imam of the Muslims after the Messenger of Allah (S).

for my Lord has sent me to teach them. Of them are: To forgive he who has oppressed you, To give to he who has deprived you, To make bonds with he who has severed from you, and to visit he (when ill) who does not visit you (when you are ill)"

Imam Ali[69] (A) in his will to Muhammad ibn al-Hanafeyyah states: *"Make sure that your brother is not stronger in his abandonment of you than your endeavour to keep your bond with him, and that he is not more persistent in his insult tc you than your kindness to him."*

Imam Saadiq (A) is reported as saying: *"The magnanimity of us the Ahl-ul-Bayt is to forgive he who oppresses us."*

The above is a small sample of the enormous collection of traditions reported in this respect.

War Conducts: Islam vs. Others

As an insight into the "Islamic wars", with a view to study the violence or the non-violence of them, a quote is made from the book "*The Phenomenon of the Spread of Islam*". The author of this book states:

> "History books which study the battles and wars over the course of history reveal that violence is an inherent phenomenon in wars. When the armies invade a country, atrocities are their normal practice. They know no mercy or compassion, they do not respect women, they do not distinguish the young from the old, and even animals and trees are not spared. This is because their aim is vengeance and revenge, and to quell any voice which opposes them. And these are not only the characteristics of invading armies, who act for economical and political objectives, but that kind of violence has even prevailed in some pre-Islamic religions.
>
> In Deuteronomy 13:15-16 we read:
>
> *"15 Thou shall surely smite the inhabitants of that city with the edge of the sword, destroying it utterly, and all that is therein, and the cattle thereof, with the edge of the sword.*

[69] Imam Ali (A), also known by his exclusive title *Amir-ul-Mu'mineen*, is the first infallible imam of the Muslims after the Messenger of Allah (S).

16 And thou shall gather all the spoil of it into the midst of the street thereof, and shall burn with fire the city, and all the spoil thereof every whit, for the LORD thy God: and it shall be a heap for ever; it shall not be built again."

And in Deuteronomy 20:11-16 we also find:

"11 And it shall be, if it make thee answer of peace, and open unto thee, then it shall be, that all the people that is found therein shall be tributaries unto thee, and they shall serve thee.

12 And if it will make no peace with thee, but will make war against thee, then thou shall besiege it:

13 And when the LORD thy God hath delivered it into thine hands, thou shall smite every male thereof with the edge of the sword:

14 But the women, and the little ones, and the cattle, and all that is in the city, even all the spoil thereof, shall thou take unto thyself; and thou shall eat the spoil of thine enemies, which the LORD thy God hath given thee.

15 Thus shall thou do unto all the cities which are very far off from thee, which are not of the cities of these nations.

16 But of the cities of these people, which the LORD thy God doth give thee for an inheritance, thou shall save alive nothing that breathe:"

In chapter 58 of his momentous book *"The Decline and Fall of the Roman Empire"*, Edward Gibbon states:

"The First Crusade recorded, in the history of mankind, the most brutal prejudice not only against the Muslims, but also against the Eastern Christians and Jews. Once they took control of the holy city of Jerusalem, the Crusaders, who saw themselves as the servants of the Lord, decided to honour their Lord by offering a bloody sacrifice to the God of the Christians . . . they slaughtered more than 70,000 Muslims! In the process neither age nor sex could mollify their implacable rage: the savage heroes of the cross indulged themselves three days in a promiscuous massacre; and the infection of the dead bodies

produced an epidemical disease. They smashed the heads of the children against the walls, threw the infants from the top of the city walls, grilled the men on fire and the Jews had been burnt in their synagogue. They ripped the bellies of pregnant women to check if they had swallowed their gold. They did not stop until they were totally exhausted. The papal envoy witnessed this genocide as he too took part in this victory."[70]

The famous historian, *Ibn Atheer*, 1160-1234, reports: *"The Europeans slaughtered more than 70,000 in the al-Aqsa mosque. Many of those murdered were women and children, as well as many Muslim imams and scholars, worshipers and pilgrims who had come from far a field to this holy site. In the rampage, the Crusaders then plundered the mosque of its countless precious jewellery."*

This kind of barbarity in war continues to this day. The wars of this (twentieth) century are gruesome examples of death and destruction. What happened in Hiroshima and Nagasaki are evidence to that, and the Zionists' atrocities in Palestine and the Lebanon are other proofs that in the mind of non-Muslims war means annihilation and destruction, which knows no mercy and kills the combatant and the civilian population alike.

As for the Muslims, the meaning of war and their understanding of it is based upon the teachings of their religion; the religion of brotherhood, equality, truth, justice and respect for the humanity of mankind. Therefore, in their wars they - the Muslims - were furthest of all people from violence and destruction. This is because a true religion does not instruct its followers to practice vengeance and revenge, but it teaches them to defend themselves and their values within the limits of humanity. The Islamic history is full of examples of Islamic ethics in war. In these scenes one can see the manifestation of humanity in the full meaning of the word, and can see mercy in various forms. In fact those scenes were, amongst many others, the reasons that attracted the people to accept Islam in their masses. See how the people of Jordan addressed the Muslim army when it arrived and camped in Jordan. They wrote:

---

[70] Edward Gibbon, 1737-1794, "*The Decline and Fall of the Roman Empire*", Chapter 58.

"O Muslim folk! We prefer you to the Romans and like you more than them, despite the fact that they have the same religion as we do. You are more faithful to us and kinder to us than them. You are least oppressive and better guardian over us. But they (the Romans) invaded us and deprived us of our rights and of our houses."

The objective of the Muslims was not to force others to accept Islam, and if the Messenger of Allah (S) wanted to adopt such a policy, he would not have sanctioned treaties and signed agreements with the Jews in Medina. What would have prevented him (S) from forcing the Jews to accept Islam or from exterminating every one of them? He (S) was the head of state, and the Muslims were the strongest force in the Arabian Peninsula. There was nothing to prevent him from doing so except the divine instruction:

"There is no coercion in religion."[71]

When the Messenger of Allah (S) arrived in Medina he sanctioned a treaty with the Jews there which states: " . . . *The Jews of 'Bani Awf' tribe are (part of) one community (together) with the (Muslim) faithful. The Jews practice their religion and the Muslims practice their own. For them shall be their own wealth, property and their persons. Except for he who has committed oppression or transgression . . .*"

This is the freedom of belief in Islam, which is manifested in the conduct of the Messenger of Allah (S). Another example is the pact that the Messenger of Allah (S) gave to the Christians of the Najraan district of Yemen. According to this pact, the Messenger of Allah (S) promised them that *they may live in the care of Allah and the protection of His messenger with their wealth, land, religion and selves fully safeguarded.* Furthermore *there will be no interference with the positions and appointments of bishops, monks, and ministers. In any dispute amongst themselves, if raised to the prophet, they will be dealt with according to fairness and justice without any injustice being incurred on any side.*

---

[71] The holy Qur'an: The Heifer (2): 256.

One of the best proofs and strongest evidences that Islam spread through persuasion, conviction and through reason, and that the sword had no role to play in the spread of Islam, is the events of the seventh century Hijri (13th century AD). These events destroyed the Islamic entity and existence and demolished the Islamic government. These were the consequences of the invasions of the Muslim state by the *Moguls* and the *Tatars*. They killed and mutilated whomever they came across, and plundered everything they could get their hands on. They destroyed every city, town, and village that they entered and annihilated every sign and symbol of civilisation that the Islamic state had instituted. These colossal events were the greatest catastrophe ever seen by the Muslims if not by humanity at large.

The famous historian *Ibn Atheer,* 1160-1234, states: *"Several years passed by and I could not find the strength to write about the colossal catastrophe for it is not within the power of any writer to write about these atrocities. There are simply not enough words to describe these horrendous events. It is not possible to give graphic details of these most horrific sufferings of Islam and Muslims. Is there anyone who can write about this? I wish I was not born or I wish I had died before this catastrophe.*

However, many friends insisted that I write at least a few words about this greatest tribulation. I was hesitant at first, but I thought that ignoring their advice would be of no use, this attempt (to write) constitutes writing about a momentous event and an almighty catastrophe the like of which the days and nights would never see again. It affected humanity in general and the Muslims in particular. If someone said that from the time that Allah created Adam until now the world had not suffered such genocide, he would be right. History books do not show any event which come anywhere near this mass murder and destruction."

Despite the fact that the Moguls slaughtered many millions of Muslim people and razed several hundred cities, towns and villages, they did not manage to quench the flame of Islam in the hearts of the remaining Muslims. In fact, and this is the point of this article, these very Muslims, who had been severely defeated, managed to beat the Buddhist and Christian missionaries to win over the hearts and minds of those nomads who practiced Shamanism.[72] It only took a few years filled with debates and discussion which took place between the supporters of each religions until those few whose power and might, and very existence had been broken by the Moguls were able to attract to Islam those ferocious conquerors. In doing so they (the Muslims) destroyed all the myths and accusations propagated by the adversaries of Islam that it is a religion that spread and survived by the sword."

Islamic Teachings on Non-violence in Combat

I would add: It is evident from the above quote that the Muslims did not have a sense of vengeance against their oppressors, as taught by the Messenger of Allah (S). This was the kind of behaviour and attitude the Messenger of Allah (S) had shown towards his enemies whether during war times or any other times. For the benefit of the reader some of the reports are presented here.

In a tradition it is reported that Imam Saadiq (A) said:

> *"Before dispatching a squadron, the Messenger of Allah (S) used to call everyone involved to a meeting and brief them about their duties and responsibilities saying: "Advance in the name of Allah, by the name of Allah, in the cause of Allah and in accordance with the religion of the Messenger of Allah (S). . . . Do not handcuff or tie up (the prisoners), Do not mutilate, Do not use treacherous means (with the enemy), Do not kill the old, Nor the young, Nor the women, Do not cut down the trees; unless you are forced to do so. If any of the Muslims, whether high ranking or otherwise, give temporary refuge to any of the infidels to hear the message of Allah (to accept Islam), (let him do so). If he follows you, (i.e. accepted Islam) then he is your brother in religion, and if he refuses, secure his safety, and seek help from Allah.""*

---

[72] Shamanism is a primitive religion practiced in northern Siberia. It believes in a hidden world belonging to the gods, devils and the spirits of the ancestors and that their priests, Shaman, practice magic to cure illness amongst others. Some sects of the red Indians in the Americas also practiced shamanism.

In another tradition, Imam Saadiq (A) is also quoted as saying:

> *"Before their mission the Messenger of Allah (S) used to order the squadron leader in particular, and the whole company in general, to fear Allah. The Messenger of Allah (S) then used to say to them: "Advance in the name of Allah and in the way of Allah. Fight any system who denies Allah, Do not use treacherous means (with the enemy), do not handcuff or tie up (the prisoners), do not mutilate, do not kill the young, nor he who has sought refuge to the peak of the mountain, do not burn the palm trees, nor flood them, do not cut down fruit-bearing trees, do not burn the crops, you may even need them, do not kill the animals except those you need to eat. Then when you meet the enemies of the Muslims invite them to one of three. If they respond (positively) to these, accept (their response) and stay your hands from them. 1. Invite them to Islam, and if they enter Islam accept it from them and stay your hands. 2. Invite them to emigrate (to Islamic cities[73]) after they have accepted Islam. If they do, accept it from them and refrain from any measures against them, and if they refuse to emigrate to such centres, they will be treated like any other Bedouin faithful; they will not qualify for Fay' and Qassma[74] rewards unless they emigrate in the cause of Allah. 3. If they refuse these two options, invite them to pay tribute submissively[75]. If they agreed to pay tribute, accept it from them, and if they refuse, then seek assistance from Allah the Almighty against them."*

While addressing the people in (preparation for the battle of) Siffeen, *Amir-ul-Mu'mineen* (A) said,

> *"Allah the Almighty has shown you a trade which delivers you from painful punishment and guides to the good; (That is) belief in Allah and struggle in the cause of Allah. He has made his reward the forgiveness of sin and beautiful dwellings in the heavens. The Almighty said:* ***"Allah loves those who fight in His cause arrayed in battle, as though they were a compact structure."*** *So make your arrays like compact structures.*

[73] This is so that they will have access to the sources of learning in those cities to educate themselves to an acceptable level. In rural and remote locations such opportunities of learning were not available at the time being.

[74] These are government income from spoil of war and land rent.

[75] The holy Qur'an: Repentance (9): 29.

> *Amir-ul-Mu'mineen* (A) continued until he said: *"Do not mutilate the dead, and if you overwhelm the enemy do not violate their properties (i.e. respect their privacy), Do not enter a house, do not take anything from their property (belongings) except what you find in their barracks. Do not agitate any woman, even if they swear at you or insult your leaders or your reverend people. For they lack the maximum physical, psychological or mental strength. We used to be instructed to refrain (from causing harm to them) even when they were idolaters. Even (at that time) if a man hit a woman he would have been rebuked and ridiculed by others (and branded as coward for using force against the weaker sex) as well as his sons.*

After the battle of the *'Camel'* was started and headed by A'ishah against Amir-ul-Mu'mineen Imam Ali (A), during which A'ishah and her army were defeated, Imam Ali (A) announced:

> *"Do not kill the injured, Do not pursue those fleeing, Whoever puts down his weapon is safe (from being attacked)."*
>
> Imam Ali (A) then rode on the mule of the Messenger of Allah (S) and called a number of individuals by name. Some 60 elders, all of whom were from the Hamdaan tribe, gathered around him wearing their protective helms, swords and shields. They followed Imam Ali (A) until he reached a big house. He asked for the door to be opened. Once inside Amir-ul-Mu'mineen saw women wailing and weeping. When they saw Imam Ali (A) they all shouted with one voice: *He is the killer of our beloveds.* Imam Ali did not say anything to them. He only asked for A'ishah's apartment. When Imam Ali entered her room, their conversation could be heard. A'ishah was apologising to Imam Ali (A). As Imam Ali (A) left the room he saw a woman who he recognised and said to her: *If I were the killer of the loved ones I would have killed those in this room, and in this room, and in this room, pointing to three different rooms.* The woman, Safeyyah, went to the wailing women to convey what Imam Ali had said. Then they all ceased wailing. Al-Asbagh, the narrator of this report, said: *In one of the three rooms was A'eshah and her entourage, in the second was Marwaan ibn al-Hakam and the youths of Quraysh, and the in the third Abdullah ibn al-Zubair and his relatives resided.* Al-

> Asbagh was asked; "Why did you not arrest them? Were they not the cause of this conspiracy and the war? Why did you leave them free?" Al-Asbagh replied: *"We had reached for our swords, with our eyes focused on him (Imam Ali), awaiting his command . . . but he did not issue any order except a general amnesty."*

There are countless cases like this, but we only mentioned the above few cases to hint at this point that it is imperative for the Islamic government, and the Islamic movement before that, to adhere to non-violence, even when in power.

Weapon of Non-Violence vs. Violence

Just as violence is a weapon, non-violence is a weapon too. However, the weapon of non-violence is more effective than the weapon of violence. Just as the soul is stronger than the body, so too is non-violence, since it is the weapon of the soul, and so it is more powerful than the weapon of the body which is made of matter. For this reason, the non-violence of the prophet Abraham (A) defeated King Nimrod's violence, and Moses' non-violence defeated Pharaoh's violence, and Jesus' non-violence defeated Herod's violence, and the non-violence of the Messenger of Allah (S) defeated the violence of the pagans' great knights.

If an individual is able to use the weapon of non-violence then it is inevitable that his adversary would succumb to him no matter how strong or ferocious his enemy may be. So we see that Jesus (A) ordered his followers to offer the right cheek of their face to he who slaps them on the left. In doing so he does not want to encourage the offender but he wants to draw the offender to the territory of justice and virtue. Since such a reaction would create a powerful storm in the soul of the offender in sympathy with the victim, which in turn leads the oppressor to be humble before the oppressed. What a transcendental wisdom it is that one can sustain a continuous and satisfactory victory by enduring a little suffering and attract the intelligent foe to one's principles.

In the book *"Towards Islamic System of Government"* I have discussed this issue as follows:

Non-violence is the third stand upon which the Islamic movement bases its call for an Islamic government, and this is of utmost importance.

Non-violence requires a very strong and resilient character, which can withstand any assault with total tolerance, and without retaliating, even if the opportunity is there to do so.

Non-violence is manifested in the hand, in the tongue, and in the heart. Each is easier than the other. Non-violence of the hand is easier than that of the tongue and non-violence of the tongue is easier than that of the heart.

The meaning of non-violence is that an individual puts things right, whether constructive or destructive, with total leniency so that no one is harmed by this cure. It is in fact like the Balsam that is placed on an aching part of the body so that it is healed.

Physical Non-violence

As for physical non-violence, it is that an individual would not attempt to hurt another individual even with respect to the strongest of his adversaries and even if had the right to do so.

Allah the Almighty states: ***"and if you forgive, it is closest to righteousness"***[76].

Therefore one should not slap back his adversary if he did, and should not strike back if he did so, or use any tool or weapon in response. Of course, non-violence does not mean not protecting one's body from an incoming assault. This is self-defence and not violence, and self-defence is part of non-violence. This physical non-violence is a definite necessity for one who has no other means of ensuring the success of his mission.

In fact this was the approach of every great reformer or any intellectual aiming at a particular goal or principle. According to the teachings of Jesus (A), as well as the teachings of the infallible imams (A), one should not return a slap with a slap; but if slapped on the right cheek, one should be ready to receive another on the left. Some might say that this may encourage the offender. The reply (to this argument) would be that this would deter him. Do you see what reaction this response creates in the offender himself? Imagine that you hit someone and in response to this action, and

---

[76] The holy Qur'an, The Heifer (2): 237.

with total tolerance, he says to you that you can hit him again if you wish. Imagine what psychological reaction would result. For anyone who is doubtful about this great wisdom, needs to go no further than to consider the state of Jesus (A) who was surrounded by his adversaries while he had no option but to pursue his mission. Furthermore, what do you say about the Messenger of Allah, Muhammad (S)? Did he want to harm the people of Makkah? History bears witness that the Messenger of Allah (S) used to fully tolerate all the insults and deplorable treatments at the hands of his opponents. Abu Lahab used to pour sheep's fat on the Prophet's head while he was praying; another infidel spits in his face; another used to throw filth into his food. On one occasion, Abu Jahl's slave fractured the prophet's head with a bow; and another; and another; . . . After all this the Messenger of Allah (S) used to pray for these people saying *"O Allah, guide my people for they are ignorant."*

And this is how Noah, Lot, Abraham, and Ismael (A) were. Have you ever heard that Noah raised his hand to hit back at he who had beaten him unconscious? Or have you seen anywhere in the pages of history books that Lot responded to his people's aggression with aggression? Or that Abraham hit back in response to his uncle's attack? Or that Ismael raised his hand to hit back at he who sliced off some of his scalp? This is none other than because their mission required the adoption of a non-violent approach, the first and most immediate manifestation of which is physical.

The physical non-violence is a weapon that attracts the hearts and minds to he who advocates it, and incites the people against his adversaries. Imagine that you see someone hitting another person but the latter does not respond likewise. Who would your sympathies lie with? Siding with the oppressed is a universal reality that the great reformers have adopted in order to achieve their ultimate goal, which is reform.

Ghandi, one of the activists in the liberation of India, used to say: *"I learnt from Imam Hussain (A) how to attain victory while being oppressed."*

Not responding to an aggression on the reformer's side not only creates sympathy in the hearts of all other people, but it also brings about compassion in the heart of the aggressor. When someone assaults an individual and the aggressor does not see a similar response from his victim, his heart will be filled with mercy and leniency after being filled with anger and violence.

The invitation (to Islam) needs peace extensively, specially if superpowers opposed their call, whereas the movement possesses nothing but the truth.

Consider if an individual, who is armed with a sword, slaps an activist. If the latter were to respond in a similar manner, what is there to prevent the aggressor from using his sword to attack the activist? Which of the two scenarios are more desirable? To tolerate an assault in order to save his life and his mission, or to return the assault and lose his life and fail his mission?

Therefore we see that the Messenger of Allah (S) used to exemplify Bilaal, Sumayyah, Ammar, and others who tolerated numerous assaults from the pagans. This is not because it is wrong to return aggression, but since to return aggression for a man with a mission would defeat its cause. Therefore when Islam resorted to force, this was to prevent chaos and aggression, even though it normally offered forgiveness on many occasions when deemed not harmful. It has been mentioned previously that this (forgiveness) is based on the question of priorities. Suppose that you are in dispute with an aggressive opponent who has taken over your house. If he assaults you and you know that if you respond similarly, you would lose your argument against him and with that the possibility of getting back your house. Would it not be more prudent to keep your nerve and deal with him rationally rather than returning his assault with an assault? Rational reasoning would certainly opt for the former. This is the common ground between the verses:

"There is no coercion in religion"[77] and

"(This is) A declaration of immunity from Allah and His Messenger, to those of the Pagans with whom you have made treaties."[78] as well as other verses concerning fighting.

When a system-of-belief (religion) does not possess power or it aims to progress (to spread its message) then it would be absurd if it were to compel anyone to accept that belief, as this will bring about

---

[77] The holy Qur'an: The Heifer (2): 256.
[78] The holy Qur'an: Repentance (9): 1.

its prompt failure. On the other hand if it possessed power or it were preoccupied with important issues, then it would also be absurd to ignore those who engage and encourage corruption and tyranny.

Verbal Non-violence

As for verbal non-violence, it is far more difficult to manage than the physical non-violence. Therefore it can be seen in many cases that someone is not prepared to hit anyone or to assault him physically but he is prepared to assault him verbally and slander him. This is because often verbal (assault) is less prone to prosecution in this world, for the culprit to fear the outcome, and therefore the tongue is free to say anything unchecked. Fearing the consequences, the hand is tied since it is subject to more control then the tongue. More often than not, an individual verbally criticises the ruling regime endlessly but when in detention he receives the beatings, he does not return the assault. Needless to say, there is a difference between non-violence on principle and for the protection of belief and mission, and that of fearing more violence and assault. The latter is the condition of any weak individual in the claws of a powerful one, with the exception that only the weak individual would respond if he loses his rational reasoning, since no one in their right mind would do anything to cause himself more harm. Whereas the former is a spiritual virtue which an individual uses to save his mission and not out of fear of punishment. A non-violent individual will have a stronger character; a more composed, and in control of his conduct and has higher moral value and conscience than the aggressor.

In any case, verbal non-violence is to curb one's tongue and check one's words in order to make sure one's words do not damage the aggressor, whether his aggression was physical or verbal.

This kind of non-violence is a great virtue and it is imperative that those involved in the invitation to (Islam) practice it however rough a ride it may prove to be and however difficult it may be to control. The strongest of all those who respond likewise to aggression is he who, when faced with a barrage of insults and accusation, seeks refuge in silence and abstains from responding likewise, in the interest of the cause and progress of Islam.

Allah states in the holy Qur'an:

"Respond with that which is better, so that he, between whom and you there was animosity, shall be like an intimate friend. And none shall be accorded this rank except those who have stood fast, and none shall be accorded it except one blessed with great good fortune."[79]

Such a fortune is called a ***'great fortune'*** by the Lord of existence. Otherwise how can an individual respond to insult with praise (for the offending individual concerned), and to slander with commendation, and to belittlement with extolment, except if he was an individual who has stood fast, tolerated and persevered. Imam al-Sajjaad (A) in his prayer, known as *Makaarem al-Akhlaaq*, or the Most Noble of Ethics, says:

"O Lord have Mercy on Muhammad and his descendants . . . and help me to tender with sincerity whoever cheated me, and to reward with kindness whoever abandoned me, and to repay generously whoever denied me, and to recompense by making bond with whoever broke off with me, and to praise whoever backbite against me. Enable me to appreciate the good deed and forgive the bad deed."[80]

That is, Islam commissions a Muslim, for being a *muslim*, to give good counsel to he who cheats him, be kind to he who boycotts him, to give generously and extensively to he who denies him, to bond with he who cut him off, to praise he who slanders him. This duty is more so for a Muslim reformer who wants to clean and revive his country from intellectual, military, economical, and cultural tyranny and corruption. He needs this weapon (of non-violence) more than any other person. In fact this is the only weapon for the unarmed who is confronted by those who have armed themselves to the extent that they have drowned themselves in metal, fire, nuclear and Hydrogen bombs.

It is reported that Jesus (A) along with some of his follower came across a group of Jews, the latter insulted Jesus (A). In response to them, Jesus (A) praised them. His followers said to Jesus, *"O Spirit*

---

[79] The holy Qur'an: Well-Expounded (41): 34-35.
[80] Extracts from the supplications of Imam al-Sajjaad (pbuh) known as *Makaarem al-Akhlaaq* or "The most Noble of Ethics".

of Allah! They swear at you and you praise them!?" Jesus (pbuh) replied; *"Yes. Every one gives whatever he has."* What a great word and magnificent wisdom. He who is filled with insult and filth, nothing comes out of him except swearing and slander. And he who embodies goodness, wisdom, virtue and high moral values, emits nothing but kindness, praise and compassion. Thus was the teaching of the prophets with no difference between Abraham, Moses, Jesus and Muhammad as well as all other prophets (peace be upon them). With such a policy, their calls of reform succeeded and managed to open a way in the material world of position and power and establish themselves for as long as man has existed. When wealth and power have vanished, those teachings remain as the torch of guidance for mankind in the dark world that the tyrant and arrogant powers bring about.

If the prophets were not to arm themselves with the weapon of non-violence, their calls and missions would have been buried in their infancy by the lords of wealth and power. Consider, for example, the well-known story of Imam Hassan (A) when a man from Shaam[81] came across the Imam and started swearing at and cursing the Imam and his father (A). Imam Hassan (A) did not respond to the man and remained silent until he finished what he had started. When the man stopped his barrage of insults, Imam Hassan addressed the man a smile:

"O' Sheikh! I guess you are a stranger in this territory and you might have mistaken (me). For if you seek contentment from us, we would gratify you, and if you ask us for anything we shall give it to you, if you seek any guidance from us we shall guide you, and if you seek vehicle from us we shall arrange one for you, if you are hungry we shall feed you, if you need any clothes we shall give you them, if you are poor we shall give you money, if you have been expelled (from your hometown) we shall accommodate you, and if you have any need we shall fulfil your need."

On hearing this response from Imam Hassan (A), the man was so ashamed of his behaviour towards the Imam that he broke into tears

[81] Shaam was the district that included today's Syria, Lebanon, Palestine and Jordan.

and said: *"I testify that you are Allah's Deputy on this earth,* ***Allah knows best where He places His message***[82]*".*

Similar events have been reported in the traditions of the prophets and the infallible Imams (A) where they return insult and aggression with kindness, but are naturally beyond the scope of this brief work. However we can see the Qur'an puts forward a good framework for a philosophical and practical call to peace and non-violence:

"Invite (all) to the Way of thy Lord with wisdom and beautiful preaching; and argue with them in ways that are best and most gracious."[83]

"And when the ignorant address them, they say, "Peace!""[84]

"Do not dispute with the people of the Book but in the fairest way."[85]

"And if they turn their backs, say: "Bear witness that we are Muslims"[86]

"Hold to forgiveness; enjoin the good and turn away from the ignorant."[87]

"Do not curse those [deities] whom they call upon besides Allah, lest they wrongfully curse Allah without knowledge."[88]

"It is by a mercy from Allah that you dealt leniently with them; for had you been hard-hearted, they would have dispersed from around you. So pardon them and ask Allah's forgiveness for them."[89]

"Let them forgive and overlook: do you not wish that Allah should forgive you?"[90]

---

[82] The holy Qur'an: The Cattle (6): 124.
[83] The holy Qur'an: The Bee (16): 125.
[84] The holy Qur'an: The Criterion (25): 63.
[85] The holy Qur'an: The Spider (29): 46.
[86] The holy Qur'an: The Family of 'Amraan (3): 64.
[87] The holy Qur'an: The Heights (7): 199.
[88] The holy Qur'an: The Cattle (6): 108.
[89] The holy Qur'an: The Family of 'Amraan (3): 159.
[90] The holy Qur'an: The Light (24): 22.

Non-Violence by Heart

The third category of non-violence is that of the heart, which is the hardest of the three, (non-violence of the hand, tongue and heart).

Imam Saadiq (A) said:

> *'Removing and elimination of a mountain is easier than that of a heart from its position.'*

The meaning of the non-violence of the heart is that one does not fill his heart with violence towards foes and adversaries. And it is normal for what is in the heart to seep through to facial expression, and body language. *"One does not make any intention, but it shows in the slips of his tongue or features of his face."*, as stated in a *hadith* from Imam Ali (A). So one may take care to eradicate physical and verbal non-violence but not of the heart. Depicting such a condition a poet states:

As of the tongue, it is coated with honey
But the hearts (are) wasps and snakes

Furthermore is he who has violence in his heart able to hide his violence forever? Surely no. It is inevitable that his violence will come to the surface, even if under unusual circumstances. Hinting at this aspect, a poet states:

Secret has two windows: drunkenness and fury.

Since keeping what is in the heart hidden forever is normally impossible, according to the poet who states:

No matter what character an individual may have,
If he wanted it hidden from the people, it would (eventually) be found out.

Significance of the Heart

In order to recognise the importance of the non-violence of the heart, it is important to appreciate the significance of the heart and its role in shaping the character of the individual and his daily behaviour and conduct. In this respect many traditions have been stressed in Islam, as reflected by the teachings of the Messenger of Allah, Muhammad (S) and his impeccable descendents, the *Ahl-ul-Bayt* (A).

The Messenger of Allah (S) used to say:

> *"The heart is (like) a king who has troops. If the king turns out to be a good one, then his troops will be good too, and if the king is corrupt, his troops would follow suit."*

He (S) also used to say:

> *"If a person's heart is healthy, his body would be in comfort, and if the heart is malicious, the body would be malevolent."*

In this respect Imam al-Saadiq (A) said:

> *"Verily, the status of the heart to the body is that of the leader to the people."*

On this basis the impeccable Imams of the *Ahl-ul-Bayt* (A) used to emphasise upon the people in general, and their followers in particular, the significance and imperative need to maintain the purity of the heart from any evil; material and spiritual, and they used to caution them about hardheartedness and its consequences on one's conduct in life and therefore the harmful affects on the society in which he lives in.

Imam Baaqir (A) is reported as saying:

> *"Allah's punishment could be for the heart or the body . . . and a person could not receive a worse punishment than hardheartedness."*

Examples of the guidance given in terms of practical advice in this respect are many. The Messenger of Allah (S) is reported as saying:

> *"Beware of dispute and discord, for they disease the hearts . . . "*

Narrated from Imam al-Saadiq (A) who said:

> *"I forbid you from burying your own relatives (even by throwing a handful of earth on the body of the deceased during burial) for this brings about hardheartedness, and he whose heart is hard is distant from his Lord."*

It is reported that a man complained to the Prophet (S) about his hardheartedness, and the Prophet (S) said to him:

> *"If you wish to see your heart (become) lenient, then feed the poor, and wipe over the head of the orphan."*

Narrated from Imam Ali (A) who said:

> *"Companionship of the nobles gives vitality to the hearts."*

Intention and Conduct

Islamic teachings strenuously emphasise on the importance of purifying the hearts as well as the intentions within them. In this respect Imam Ali (A) states:

> *"He whose intention is good, his conduct would be pleasant."*

He also states

> *"Good conduct (throughout one's life), is indicative of one's good intentions."*

Furthermore Imam Ali (A) stresses that there is a direct relationship between the purity of one's heart and the soundness of his thoughts and insight, by saying:

> *"The goodness of the hearts and intentions is evidence for the soundness of visions."*

Imam al-Saadiq (A) states:

> *"What benefit is to he who presents a pleasant (behaviour) and hides a vile (intention)? Is it not that if he goes back to himself, he knows that that is not the case? Allah Almighty states:* ***'Rather, man shall witness against himself, even though he may put forth his excuses.'***[91] *Truly if the intention is valid, the conduct would be justified."*

The Imam emphasises that one cannot escape from the results and consequences of what he has hidden from others regardless of the passage of time when he says:

---

[91] The Holy Qur'an: Resurrection (75): 14-15.

"No one intends or commits something good unless Allah brings forth (something) good for him (even) after the passage of time, and no one intends or commits something evil unless Allah brings forth (something) bad for him after the passage of time."

Jihad of the Self

The *hardhearted* and the *ill-intended* individual is primed to transgress upon others and therefore non-violence in his conduct is not possible without purifying his heart and maintaining that status. For this reason, Islam devoted considerable attention to planting in the heart of the faithful Muslim all the various virtues, among which are non-transgression upon others' rights and refraining from any kind of violence in the treatment of others. Such qualities require such determined self-training and practice that are no less difficult than the hardships and dangers of the battlefields. Imam al-Saadiq (A) states:

"The Messenger of Allah (S) despatched a squadron and when they returned, he (S) said 'welcome to those who have accomplished the minor jihad and have to achieve the major jihad.' He was asked 'What is the major jihad?' The Prophet (S) said 'It is the jihad of the self.'"

In this respect Imam Ali (A) is reported as saying:

"Jihad of the self is the quality of the nobles."

Relating the jihad of the self to social affairs, as well as emphasising its role in this domain, the Messenger of Allah (S) states:

"The best of the jihad is to ensure that one does not even consider transgressing against others."

On another occasion, and along the same line, the Messenger of Allah (S) states:

"Through jihad one can overcome one's bad habits."

And also:

"Wage jihad against the desires of your selves, (and as a result) your hearts will be occupied by wisdom."

Since the resident contents of the hearts are reflected in the appearances of the faces, the Messenger of Allah (S) used to warn of the fate and destiny of he who hurts other even by the gesture of a single look:

"He who, by a single look at a believer, causes him anxiety, will be apprehended by Allah on a day when there is no protection except His. (i.e. on the Day of Judgement.)

Vice and Virtue

In a nutshell, whatever one harbours in his heart, will be manifested in his conduct and behaviour. If one wishes to lead a happy and prosperous life respecting others and being respected by them, one must ensure to avoid detestable traits, in particular those such as hatred, jealousy, rage, etc. The least results of such traits, which originate from the heart, manifest in various conducts such as clashing with others, and violent confrontations; whether physical, verbal or by heart. Imam Ali (A) states

"Jealousy does not attract anything except harm and fury, languishing your heart and sickening your body."

And

"Fury is the fire of the hearts."

Imam Saadiq (A) states,

"Rage is an annihilator of the heart of the wise man."

Imam Ali (A) states,

"The cause of commotion is hatred",

And

"The weapon of evil is hatred."

Outlining the cure for these social diseases Imam Ali (A) sates:

"He who abandons hatred will have a relieved heart."

Thus Islamic teachings clearly identify the material and spiritual consequences of harbouring disparaged attributes, and actively encourage the individual to attain virtuous qualities, one of the most important of which is forbearance. Imam Saadiq (A) is reported as saying

> *"Forbearance is a sufficient victor."*

Imam Ali (A) states

> *"I found forbearance and tolerance better victors for me than brave men."*

He also says

> *"Peace is the fruit of forbearance."*

Non-violence by heart is an extremely praiseworthy quality, but it requires resolute determination and continuous effort to attain, giving praiseworthy results to he who harbours it. If there is a starting point to everything, then the starting point for this momentous task is the guidance of Imam Ali (A) who says

> *"Eliminate evil from the heart of others by uprooting it from your heart."*

The Author

Ayatollah al-Udhma Imam Muhammad Shirazi is the Religious Authority, or *Marje'*, to millions of Muslims around the globe. A charismatic leader who is known for his high moral values, modesty and spirituality, Imam Shirazi is a mentor and a source of aspiration to Muslims; and the means of access to authentic knowledge and teachings of Islam. He has tirelessly devoted himself, and his life, to the affairs of Muslims in particular, and to that of mankind in general. He has made extensive contributions in various fields of learning ranging from Jurisprudence and Theology to Politics, Economics, Law, Sociology and Human Rights.

Muhammad Shirazi was born in the holy city of Najaf, Iraq, in 1347 AH (Muslim calendar), 1927 AD. He settled in the holy city of Karbala, Iraq, at the age of nine, alongside his father. After primary education, the young Shirazi continued his studies in different branches of learning under his father's guidance as well as those of various other eminent scholars and specialists. In the course of his training he showed a remarkable talent and appetite for learning as well as a tireless commitment to his work and the cause he believed in. His extraordinary ability, and effort, earned him the recognition, by his father and other *Marje's* and scholars, of being a *Mujtahid*; a qualified religious scholar in the sciences of Islamic jurisprudence and law. He was subsequently able to assume the office of the Marje' at the early age of 33 in 1960. His followers are found in many countries around the globe.

Imam Shirazi is distinguished for his intellectual ability and holistic vision. He has written various specialized studies that are considered to be among the most important references in the Islamic sciences of beliefs or doctrine, ethics, politics, economics, sociology, law, human rights, etc. He has enriched the world with his staggering contribution of more than 1000 books, treatise and studies on various branches of learning. His works range from simple introductory books for the young generations to literary and scientific masterpieces. Deeply rooted in the holy Qur'an and the Teachings of the Prophet of Islam, his vision and theories cover areas such as Politics, Economics, Government, Management, Sociology, Theology, Philosophy, History and Islamic Law. His work on Islamic Jurisprudence (*al-Fiqh* series) for example constitutes 150 volumes, which run into more than 70,000 pages. Through his original thoughts and ideas he has championed the causes of issues such as the family, human right, freedom of expression, political pluralism, non-violence, and Shura or consultative system of leadership.

Imam Shirazi believes in the fundamental and elementary nature of freedom in mankind. He calls for freedom of expression, political plurality, debate and discussion, tolerance and forgiveness. He strongly believes in the consultative system of leadership and calls for the establishment of the leadership council of religious authorities. He calls for the establishment of the universal Islamic government to encompass all the Muslim countries. These and other ideas are discussed in detail in his books.

Teachings of Islam

www.shirazi.org.uk

A site dedicated to the cause of Islam, Muslims and Mankind.

Islam aims to bring about prosperity to all mankind. One of the leading authorities on Islam today, Imam Muhammad Shirazi, calls upon all Muslims to adhere to the teachings of Islam in all domains in order to regain their former glory and the salvation of mankind. These teachings include:

- PEACE in every aspect.
- NON-VIOLENCE in all conducts.
- FREEDOM of expression, belief, etc.
- PLURALISM of political parties.
- CONSULTATIVE System of Leadership.
- The re-creation of the single Muslim nation - without geographical borders, passports between them, as stated by Allah:

  "This, your community is a single community and I am your Lord; so worship Me."

- The revival of Islamic brotherhood throughout this nation:

  "The believers are brothers."

- Freedom from all the man-made laws, shackles and restrictions as stated in the Qur'an:

  "... and (the Prophet Muhammad pbuh) releases them from their heavy burdens and from the shackles that were upon them."

This is the official website of Imam Shirazi. You can email your queries on issues of concern to the site at: **queries@shirazi.org.uk**

Other Publications by *fountain books*

1. *Aspects of the Political Theory of Imam Muhammad Shirazi*

Muhammad Ayub is a well-known Islamist political activist within the Iraqi circle who has established a long history of political struggle behind him. He was attracted by the views of the Imam Muhammad Shirazi in the fields of social and political sciences. This prompted the author to write this book to introduce the reader to these views that have remained relatively unknown to the Muslim activists and reformists. It covers such aspects on politics as freedom of expression, party-political pluralism and organisation, social justice, peace and non-violence, human rights, consultation system of government, etc.

2. *Islamic System of Government*

In this introductory book the author outlines the basic principles of a government based on the teachings of Islam. The author begins with the aim and objectives of the government according to Islam and the extent of its authority. He then addresses, from the Islamic viewpoint, the significance and fundamental nature of such issues as consultative system of government, judicial system, freedoms, party political pluralism, social justice, human rights, foreign policy, etc. The author also outlines the policies of a government on issues such as education, welfare, health, crime, services, etc. as well as such matters as the government's income, and authority.

3. *If Islam Were To Be Established*

This book can serve as the Muslim's guide to the Islamic government. If an Islamist opposition group has a plan for an Islamic government, this book would help to check various aspects of the plan. In the absence of such a plan, this book would present one. To the non-Muslims, the book presents a glimpse of a typical Islamic system of government. The book would also serve as a yardstick for anyone to check the practices of any government that claims to have implemented an Islamic system of government.

4. *The Family*

In this book the author highlights the problems he sees primarily in Islamic societies and particularly in the west today, from the phenomenon of unmarried young men and women through to birth control and contraception. He surveys the idea of marriage in various religions and schools of thought and discusses polygamy from the

Islamic perspective. As well as being a call to the Muslim world to revert to the true teachings of Islam, this book can also be of use as an introduction to others who seek some answers to the social problems of today. This is because Islam has detailed teachings, which promise success in every area of human life on individual and societal levels, and what's more their practicality has been historically proven.

5. *The Qur'an: When was it compiled?*

In this book the author addresses the issues of when the Holy Qur'an was compiled, on what and whose instructions was this task carried out and who accomplished its compilation in the form that it is available today. In this work the author presents undisputable evidence as to address these crucial questions. Through historical, methodical and logical analyses, the author establishes how and when the compilation of the Holy Qur'an was achieved. In the latter half of the book the author cites many Prophetic traditions on the significance of the learning and recitation of Holy Qur'an. It is a must read for every Muslim, and any non-Muslim who follows Islamic issues.

6. *Fundamentals of Islam*

In this book the author outlines the five fundamental principles of Islam, namely the Indivisible Oneness of God *(Tawheed),* Divine Justice *(Adl),* Prophethood *(Nubowwah),* Leadership of mankind *(Imamah),* and Resurrection *(Me'ad).* For each principle, the author presents a concise discussion on the significance of the issue concerned. The book could serve as a good introduction to fundamental Islamic beliefs, both for the Muslim and non-Muslim alike.

Also available from:

- www.ebooks.com
- www.amazon.co.uk

Europe

Alif International,
109 Kings Avenue,
Watford,
Herts. WD1 7SB,
UK
Tel. + 44 1923 240 844
Fax + 44 1923 237 722.

USA

TTQ, Inc.
P.O. Box 731115
Elmhurst, New York 11373
USA
Tel. + 1 718 446 6472
Fax + 1 718 446 4370

Free Muslim is an independent, humanitarian and political, Islamic organisation that strives to encourage and promote the policies of non-violence to be upheld and practiced by everyone and in all aspects of life.

Free Muslim aims to defend the values and teachings of Islam, to educate the Muslim society with the spirit of debate and respecting the opinions of others in searching for the truth.

The objectives of Free Muslim is to promote and crystallise non-violence in accordance with Islamic law, to intermediate between the nations and organisations and their Muslim governments and conciliate between them in order to safeguard the Muslim community and eliminate any traces of violence, to call for the freedom of prisoners of conscience, to call for the abrogation of the Death penalty in accordance with Islamic law, to promote and present the teachings of Islam accurately and to correct the false attributes which are made to Islam by the mass media, to promote the just peace and implement social justice throughout the world, according to the teaching of Islam.

Free Muslim
PO Box 13/5570
Beirut, Lebanon
www.freemuslim.org
freemuslim@freemuslim.org
Tel: 00 9611 275 675
Fax: 00 9611 541 483
Fax: 00 114 134 871 747 (USA)